Gone Painting

A photo art book cataloguing the paintings of Irish artist Brendan Allard

Paintings by Brendan Allard

Compiled by Gordon Allard

Text copyright © 2020 Gordon Allard

All Rights Reserved.

This is a photobook. Names, businesses, places, events and incidents are either the products of the author's imagination or used in a fictitious manner. Any resemblance to actual persons, living or dead, or actual events is purely coincidental.

To my father Brendan Allard, the man who taught me to never give up and to always pursue my dreams

Table of Contents

Forward

1. Cottages

2. Lakes and Rivers

3. Animals

4. Bridges

5. Seascapes

Forward

My father Brendan Allard was born on the 27th of June 1943 and grew up on the banks of the Royal canal near Shandonagh Bridge, Mullingar, Co. Westmeath, Ireland. He was the second youngest son of a family of five brothers and one sister. They had a farm on the banks of the canal and it was living here that my father got his love for the water and of nature in general. He worked most his life on building sites all over Ireland and even built his own house until he developed multiple sclerosis in the 1980's. He was always very talented with making things and he self taught himself how to paint even when he was suffering the debilitating effects of multiple sclerosis. He always loved life and kept going as much as he possibly could. He represented Ireland several times as a member of the Irish disabled fly fishing team and he tried to paint as much as he could as he got great enjoyment from it. He was very generous and gave away an immense amount of his paintings for free. The paintings in this book are just a small selection of what he painted and are displayed in no order. He experimented with different styles and painting techniques but his preferred paints were acrylic which is what the paintings in this book were painted with. My father loved the outdoors so most of his paintings represent his interests such as old Irish cottages, lakes, rivers, boats, fishing and the sea so I have divided his paintings in this book into five categories Cottages, Lakes and Rivers, Animals, Bridges and Seascapes. My father always wanted as many people as possible to enjoy his paintings so I hope you get some inspiration from his paintings and get pleasure from looking at them.

Gordon Allard,

Ireland, 2020.

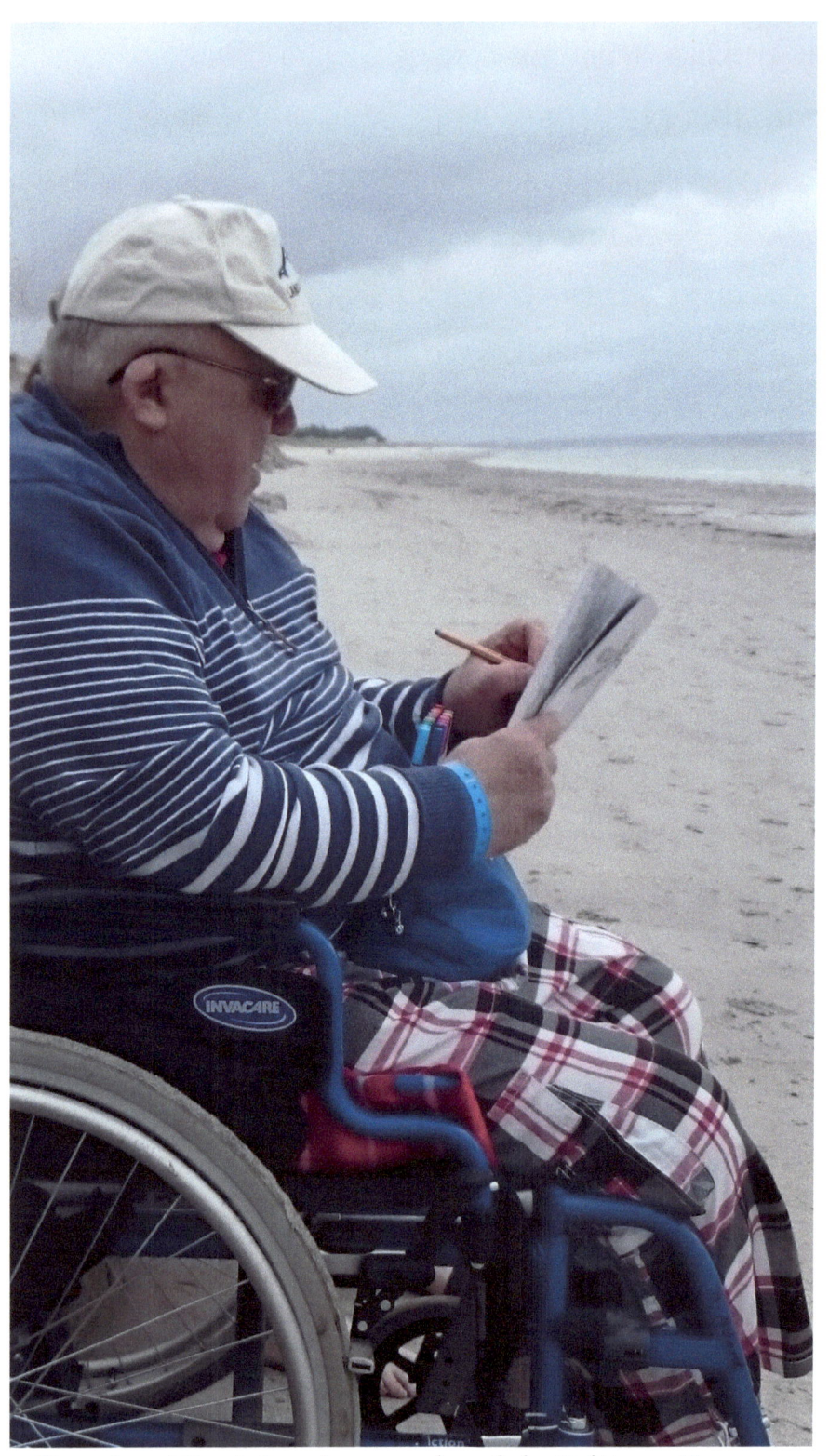

Brendan Allard drawing on a beach in Brittany, France.

1. Cottages

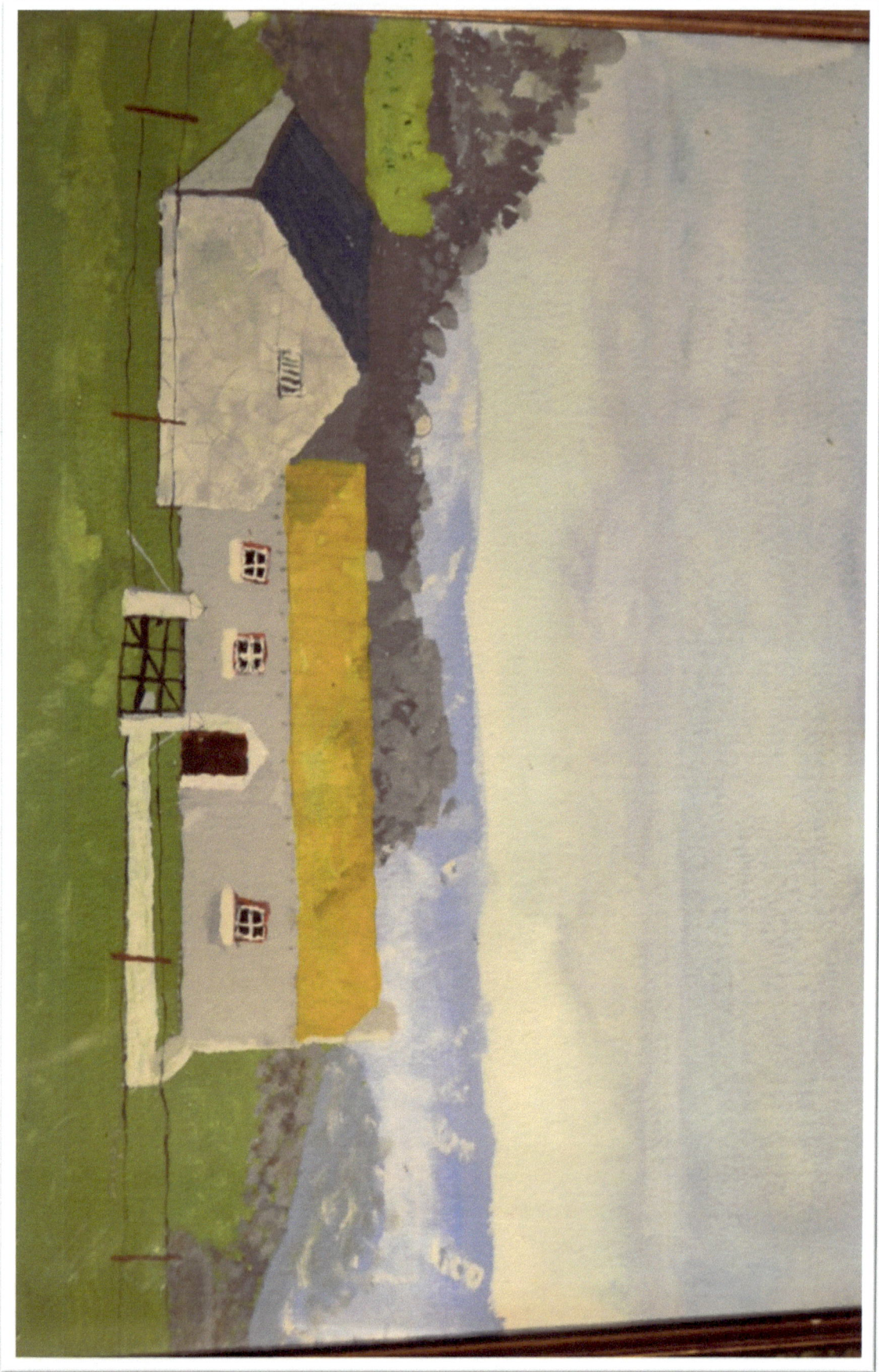

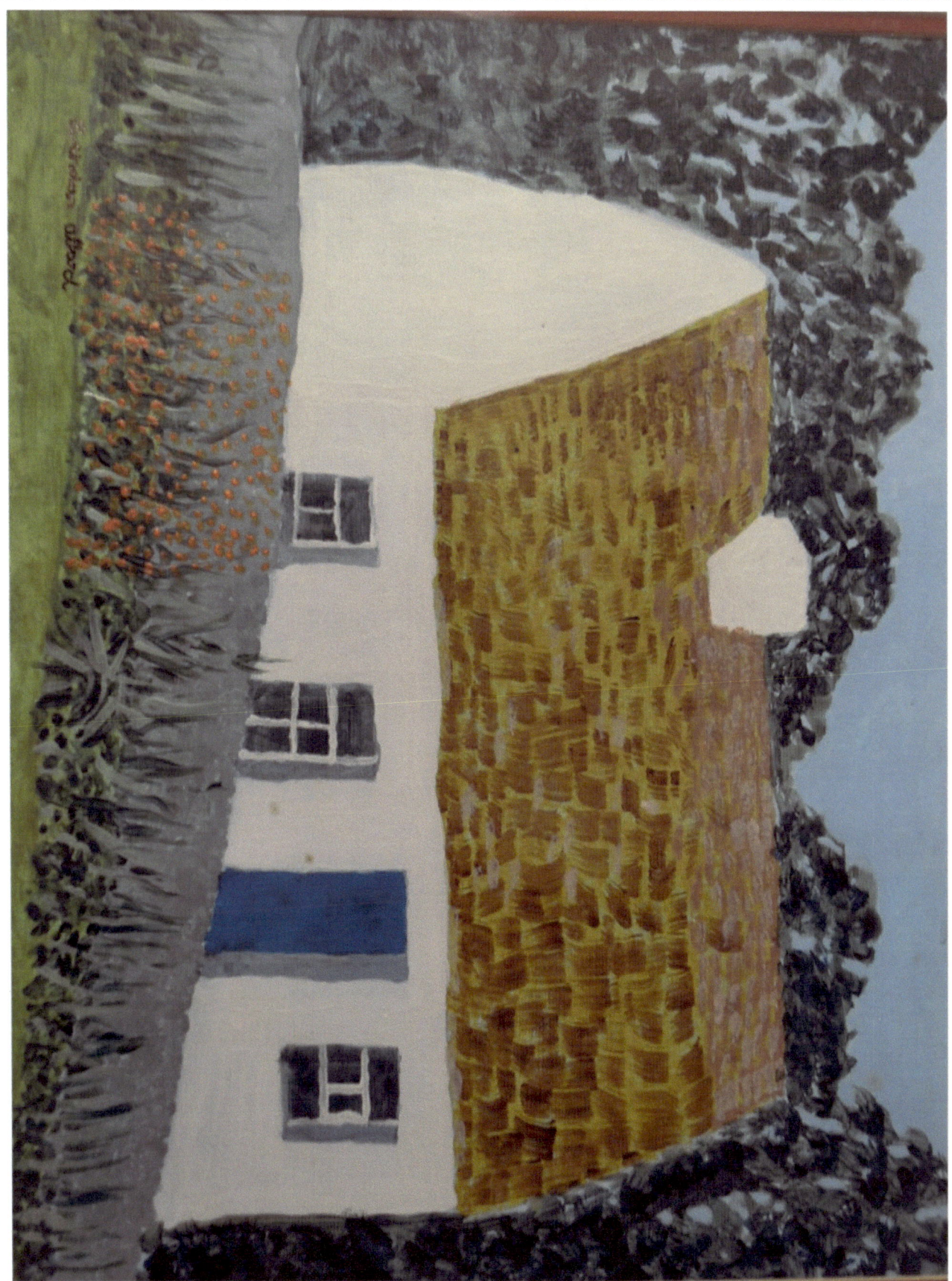

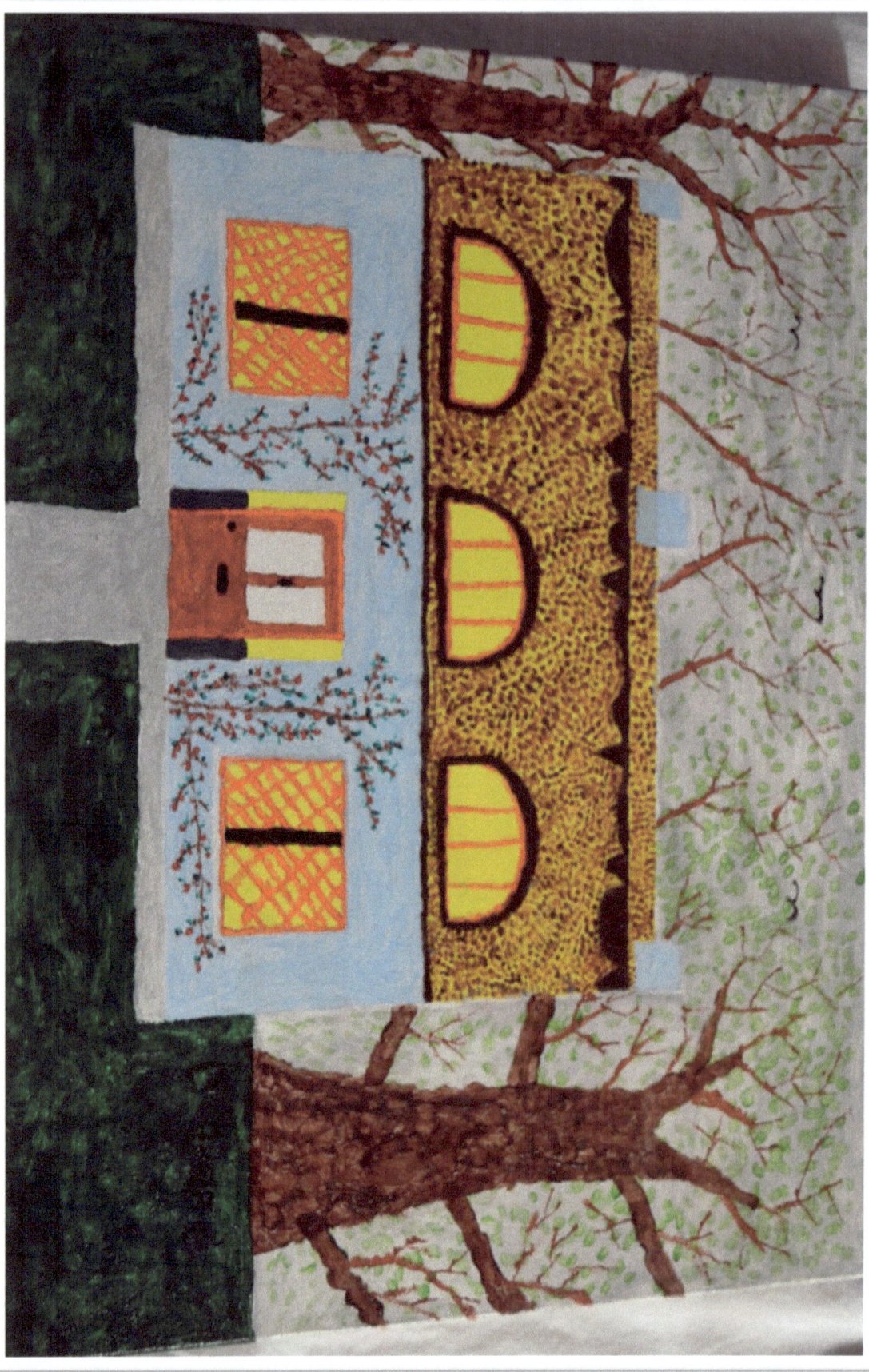

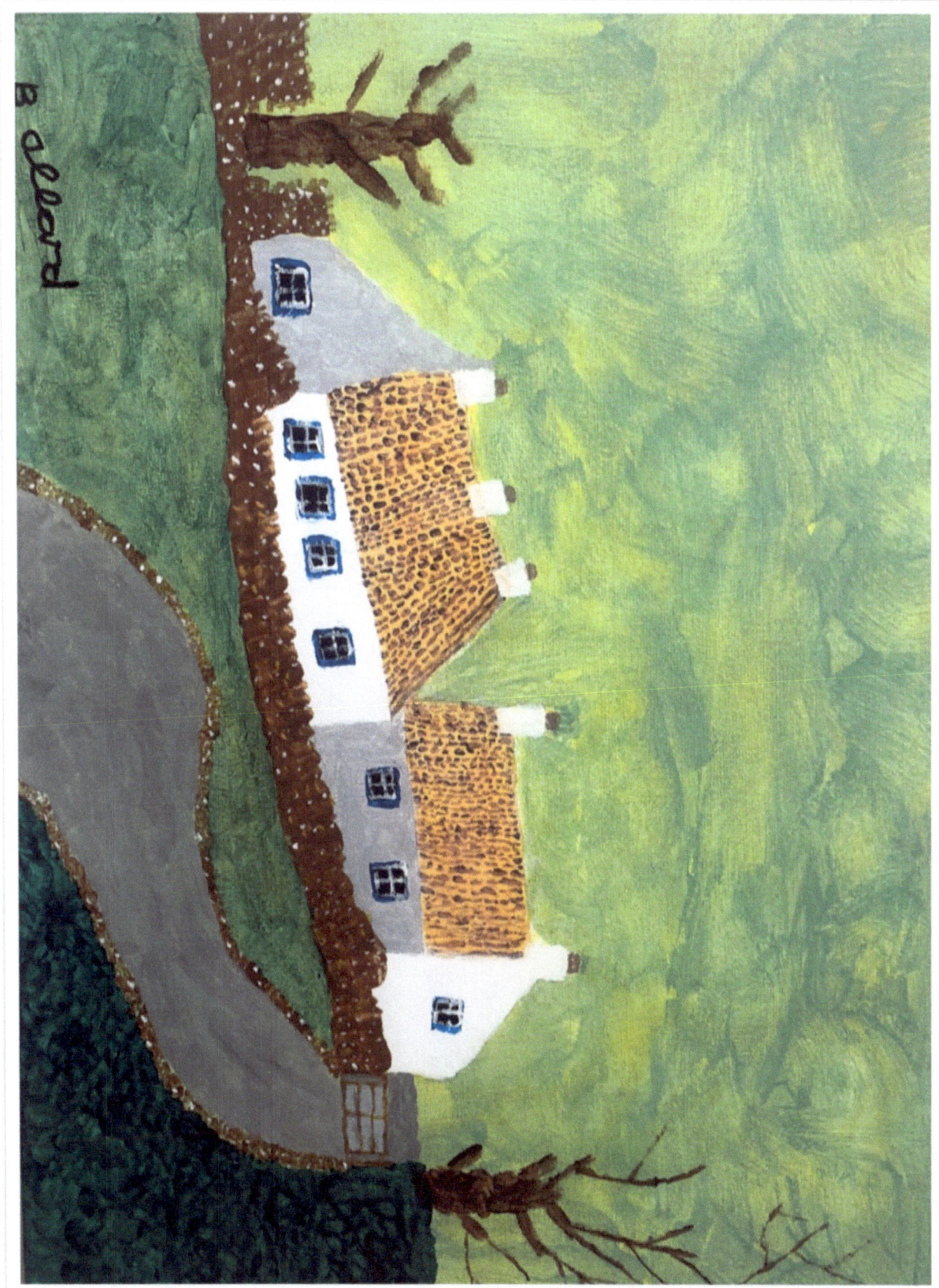

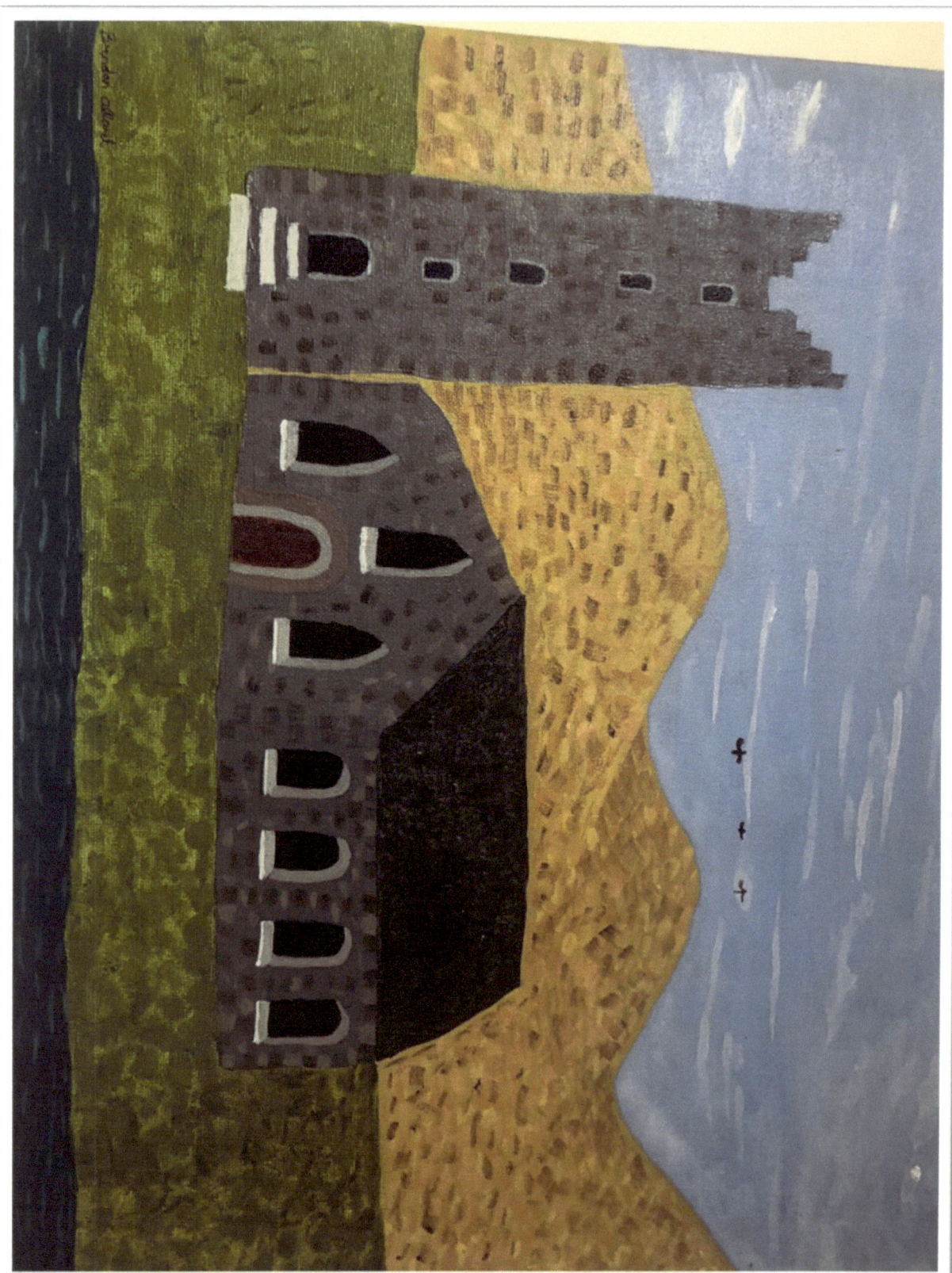

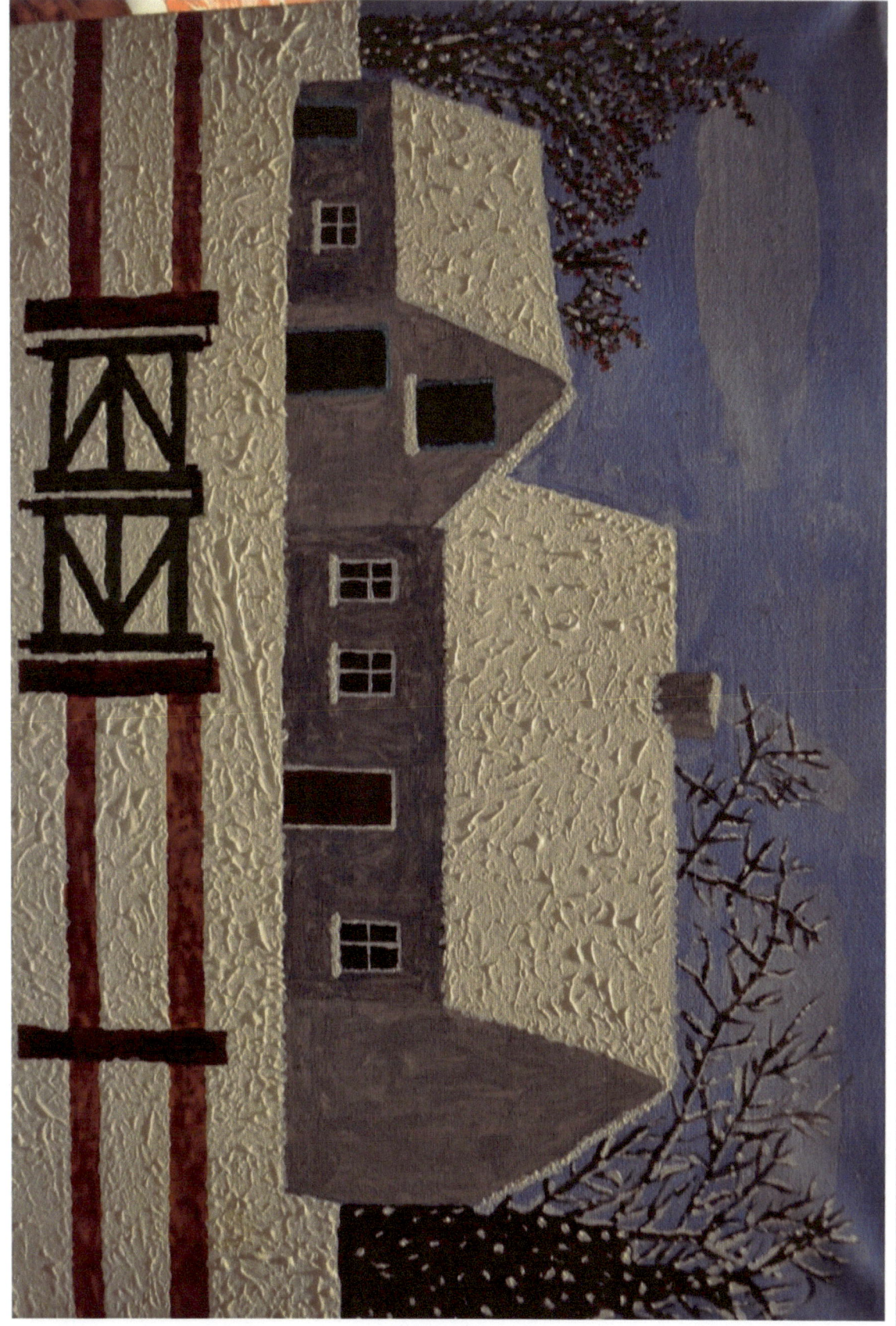

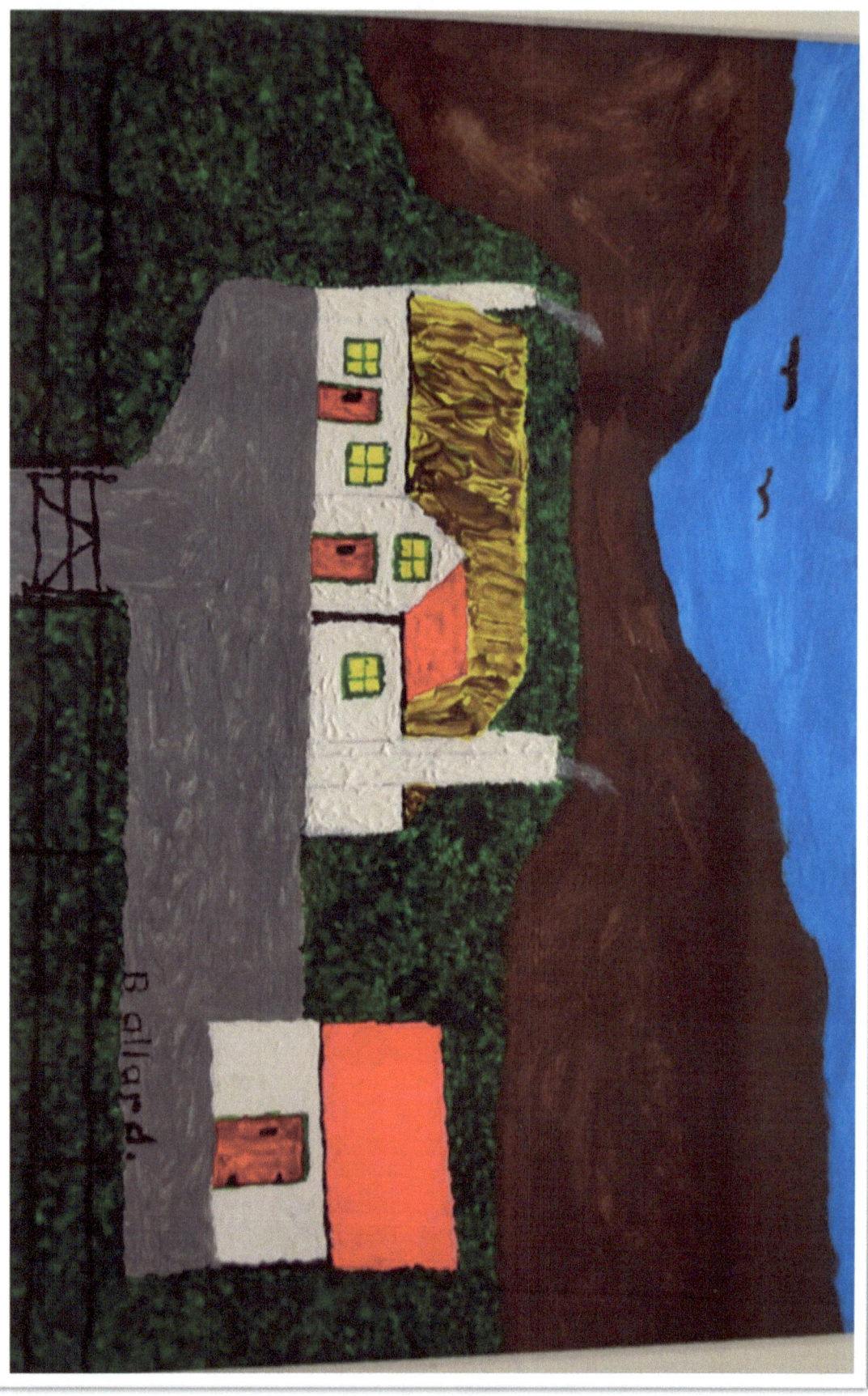

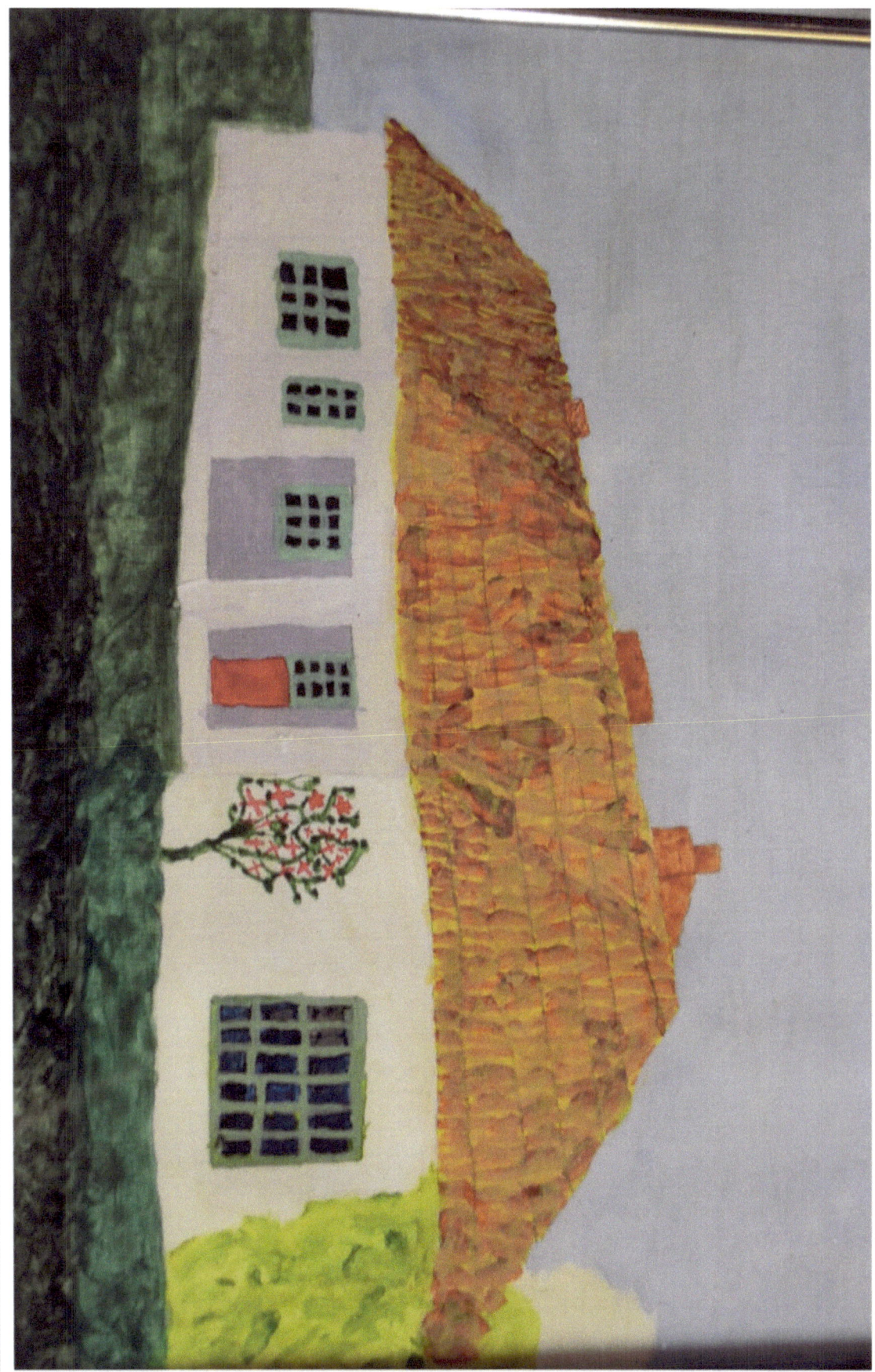

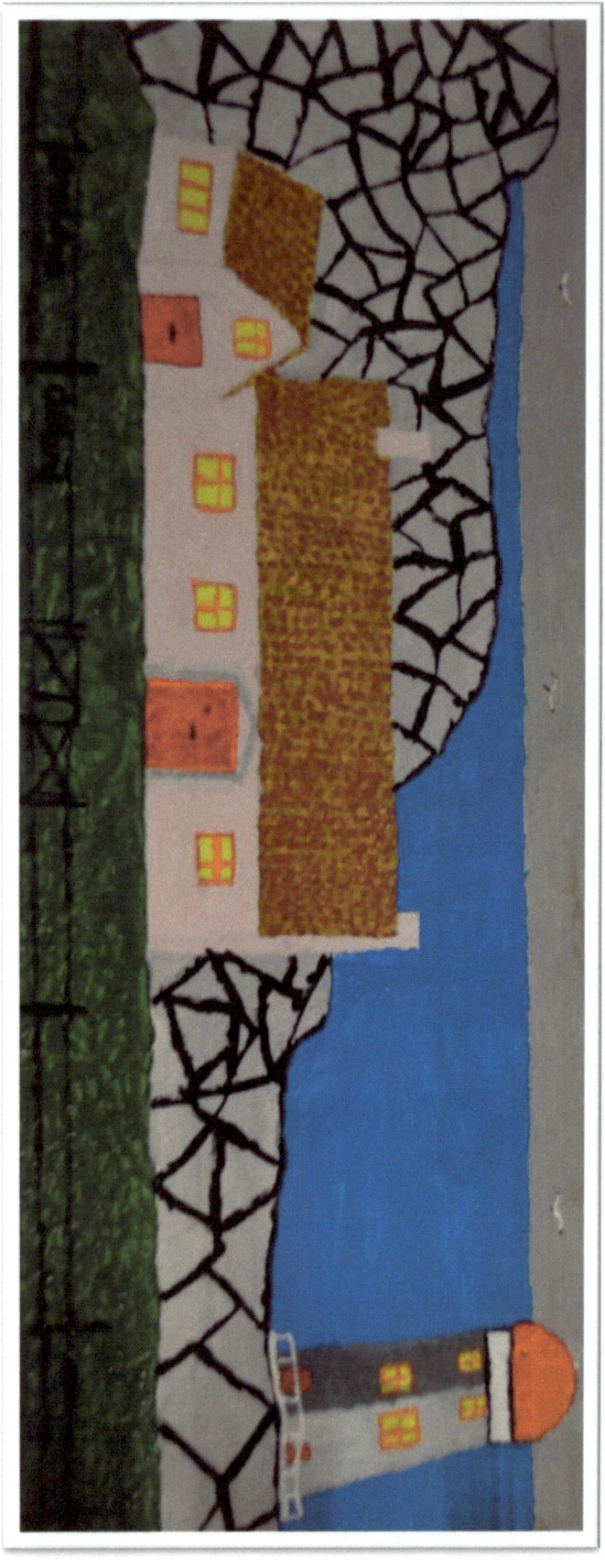

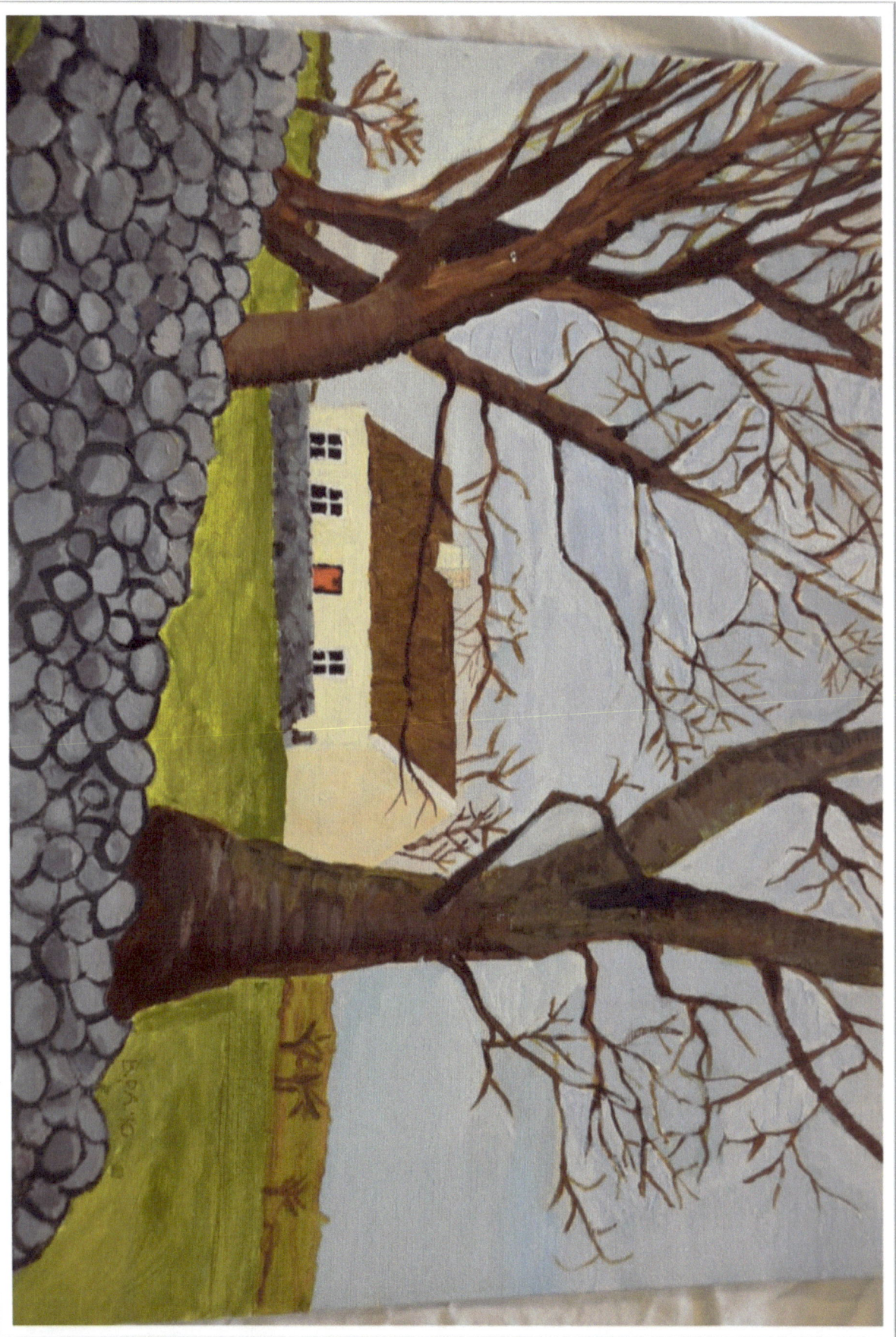

2. Lakes and Rivers

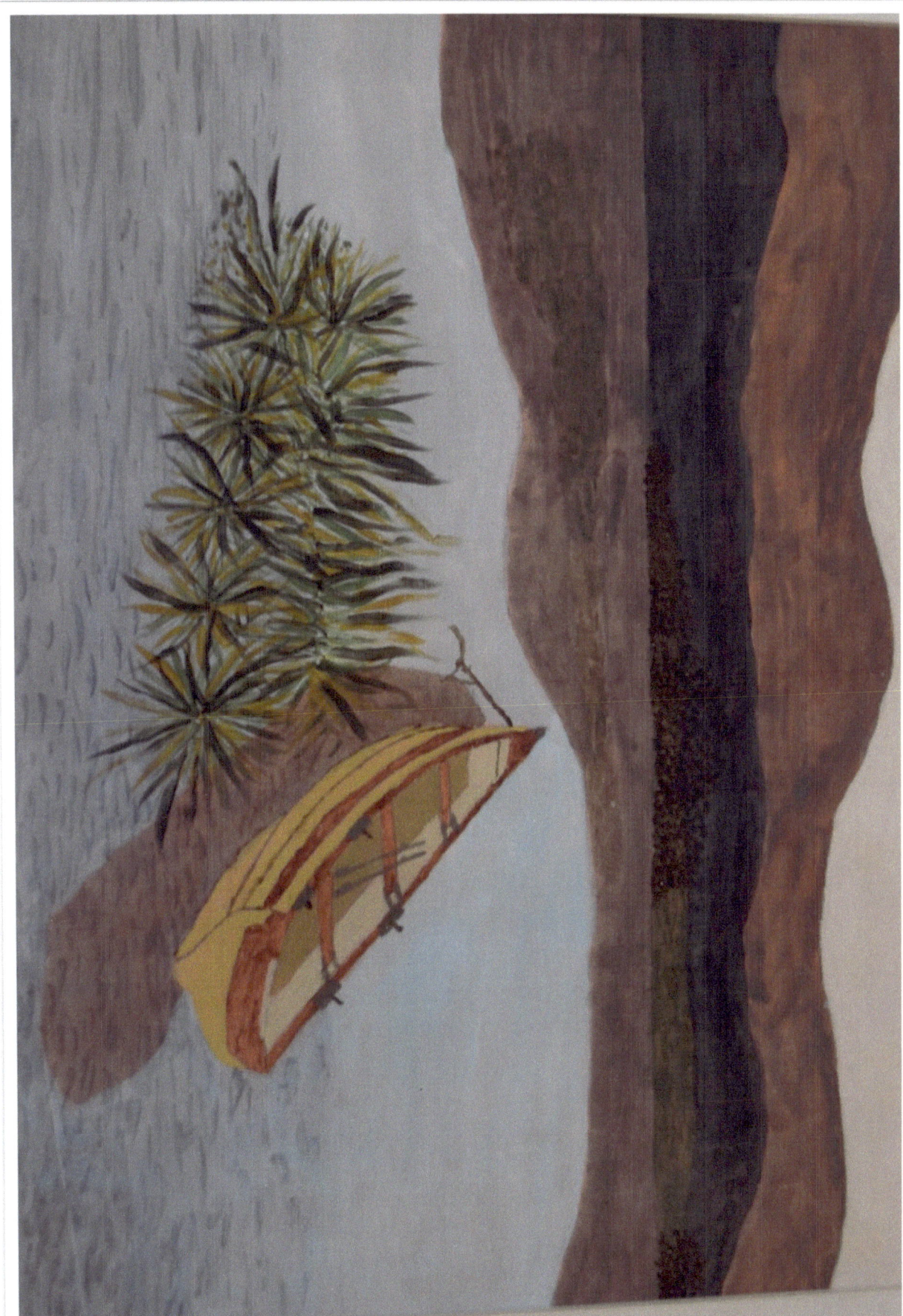

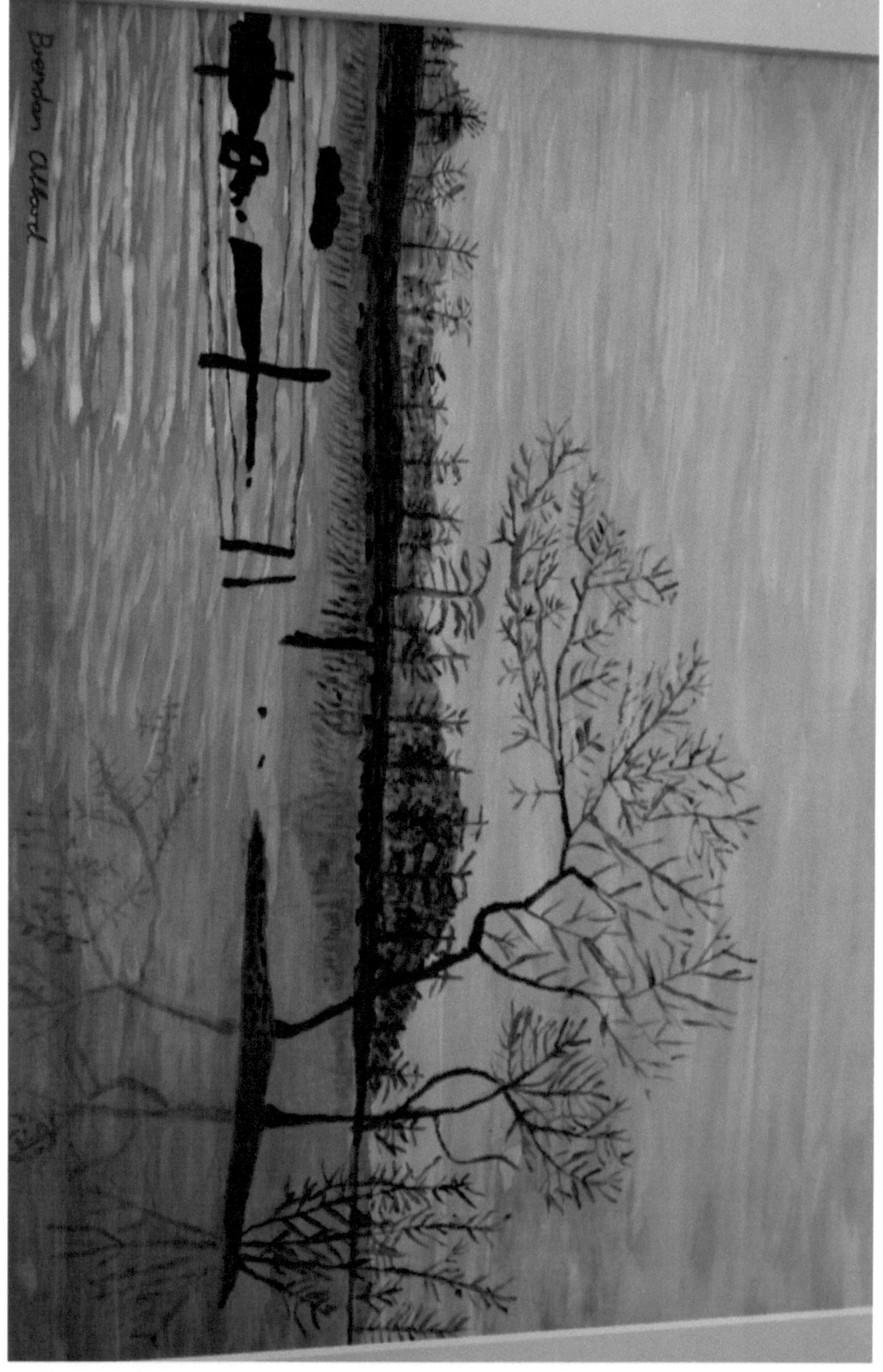

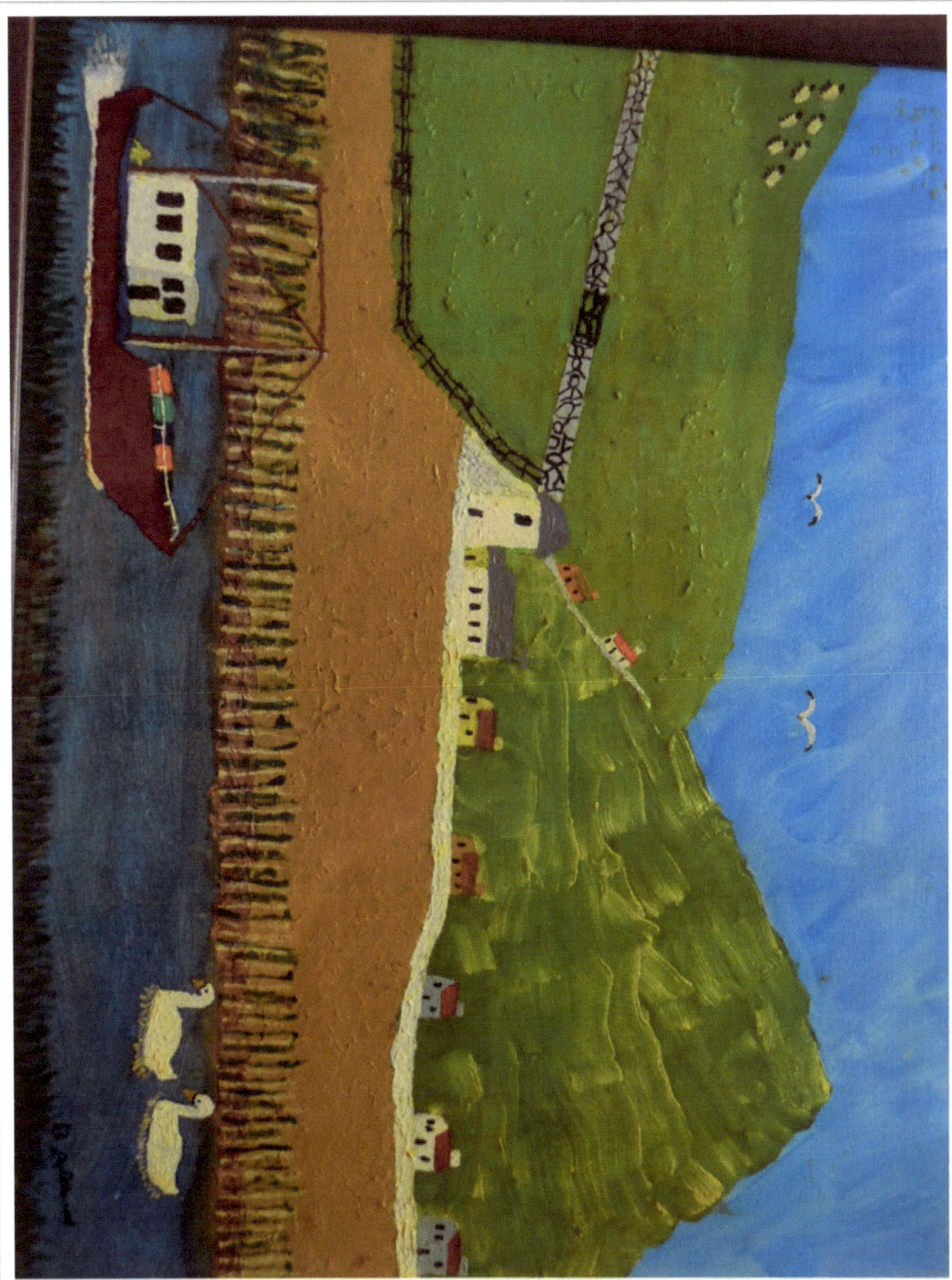

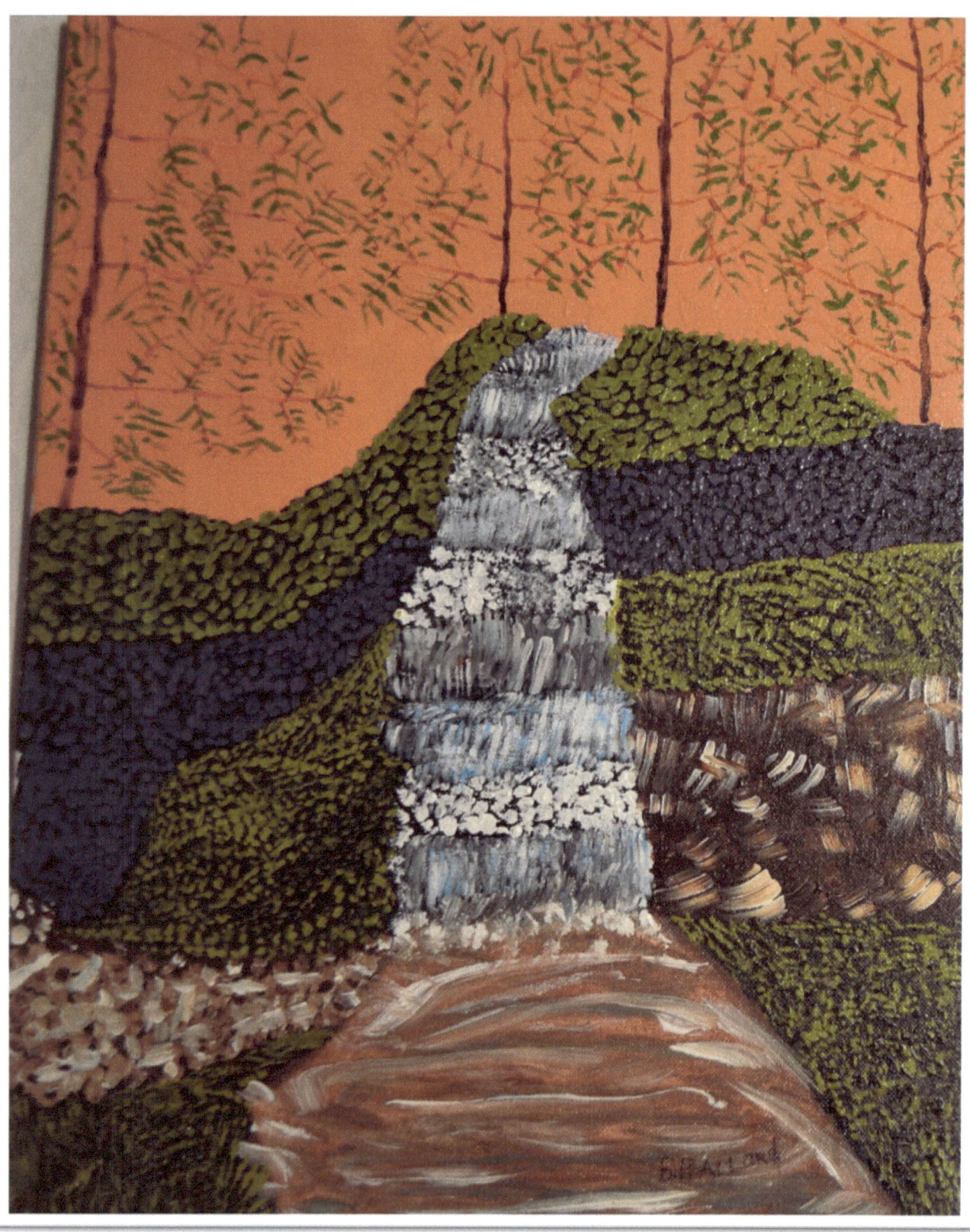

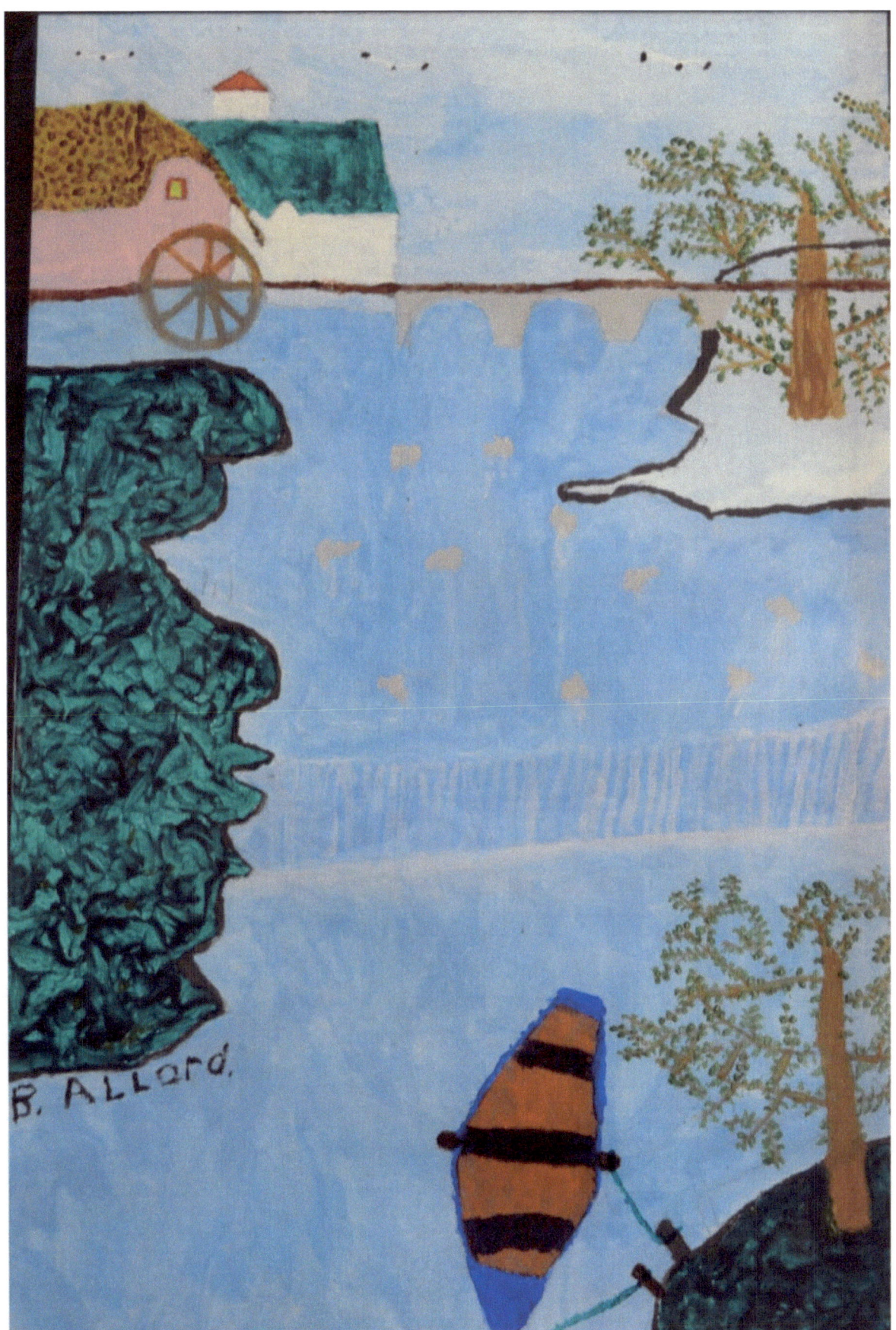

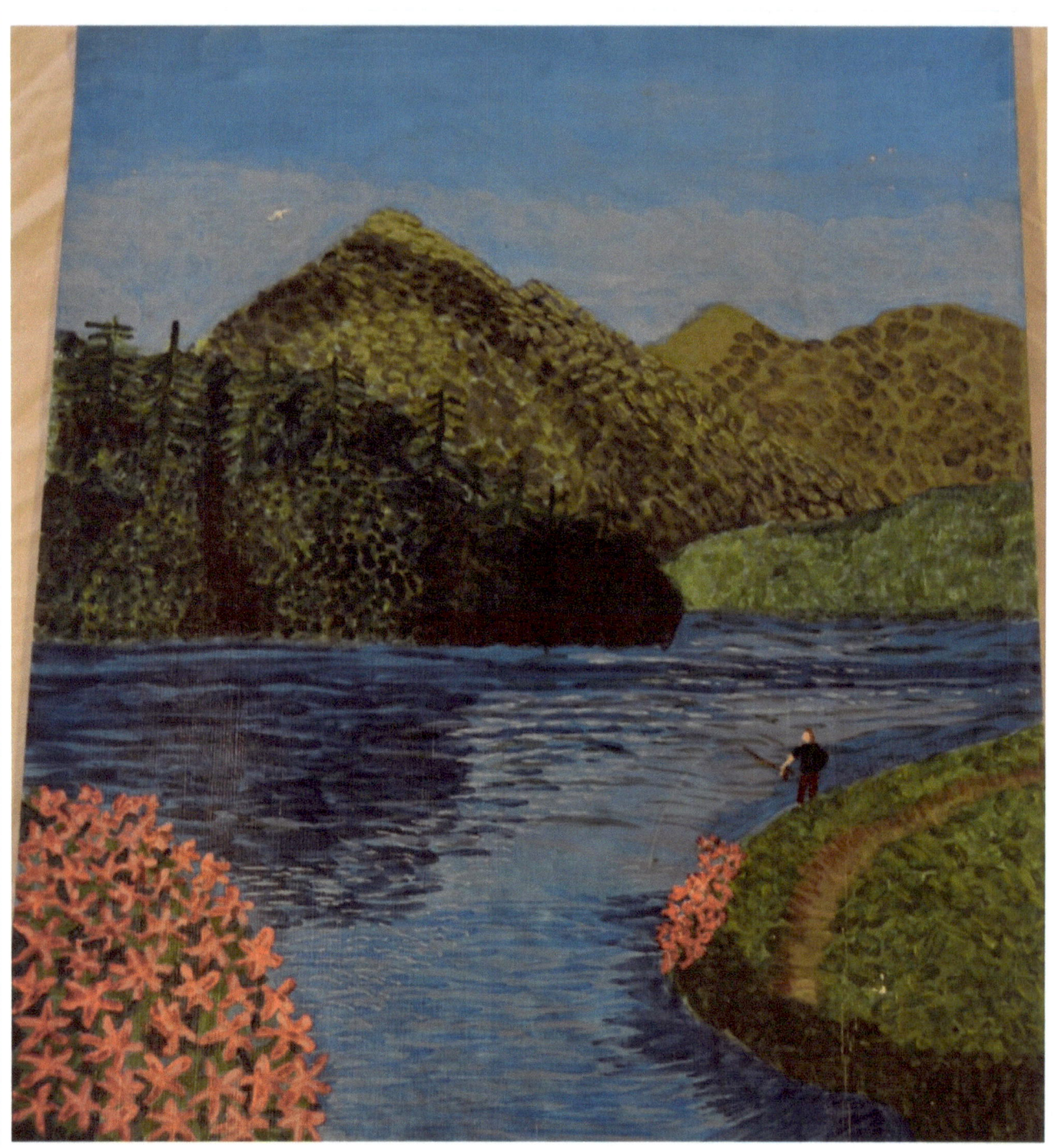

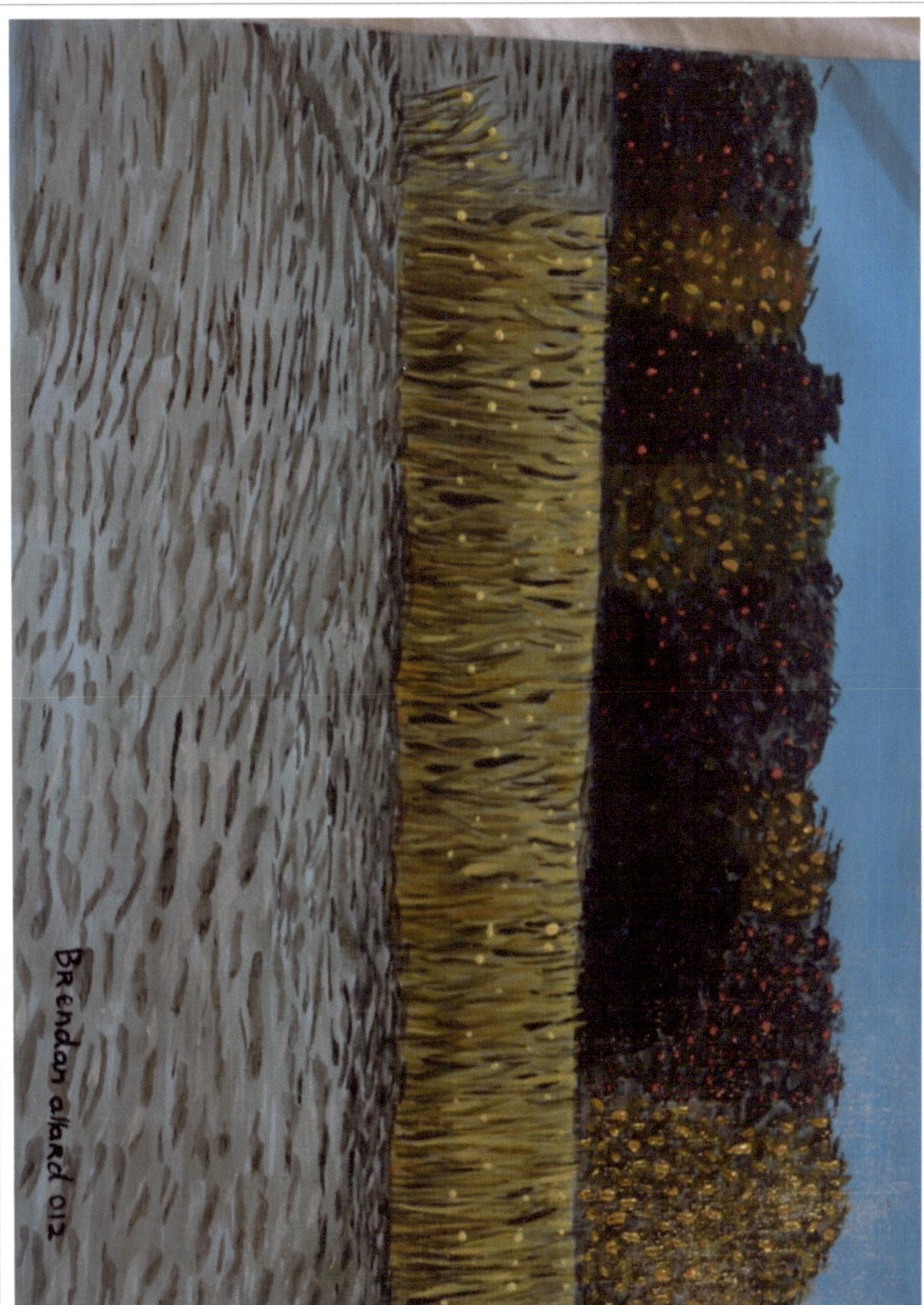

3. Animals

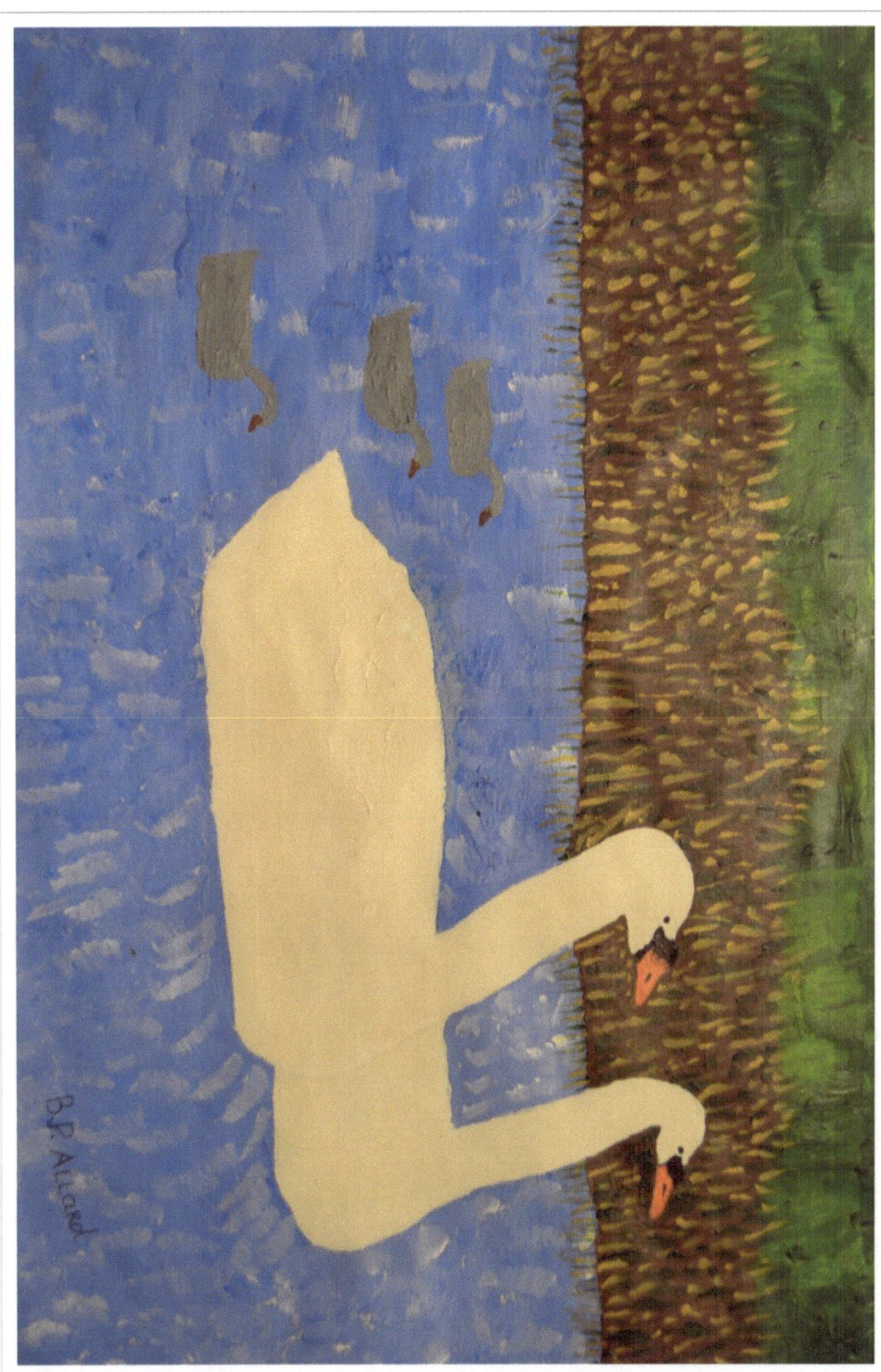

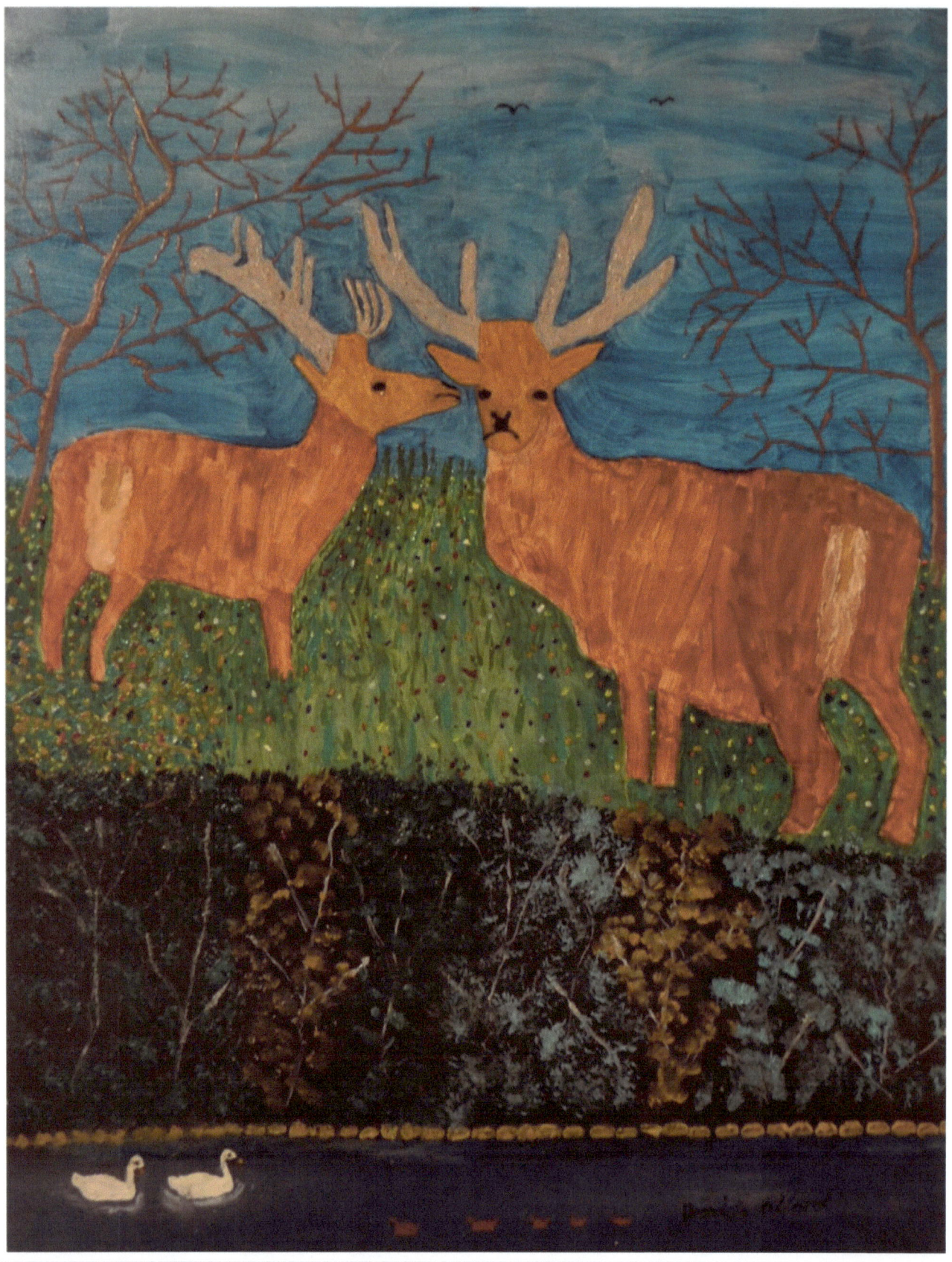

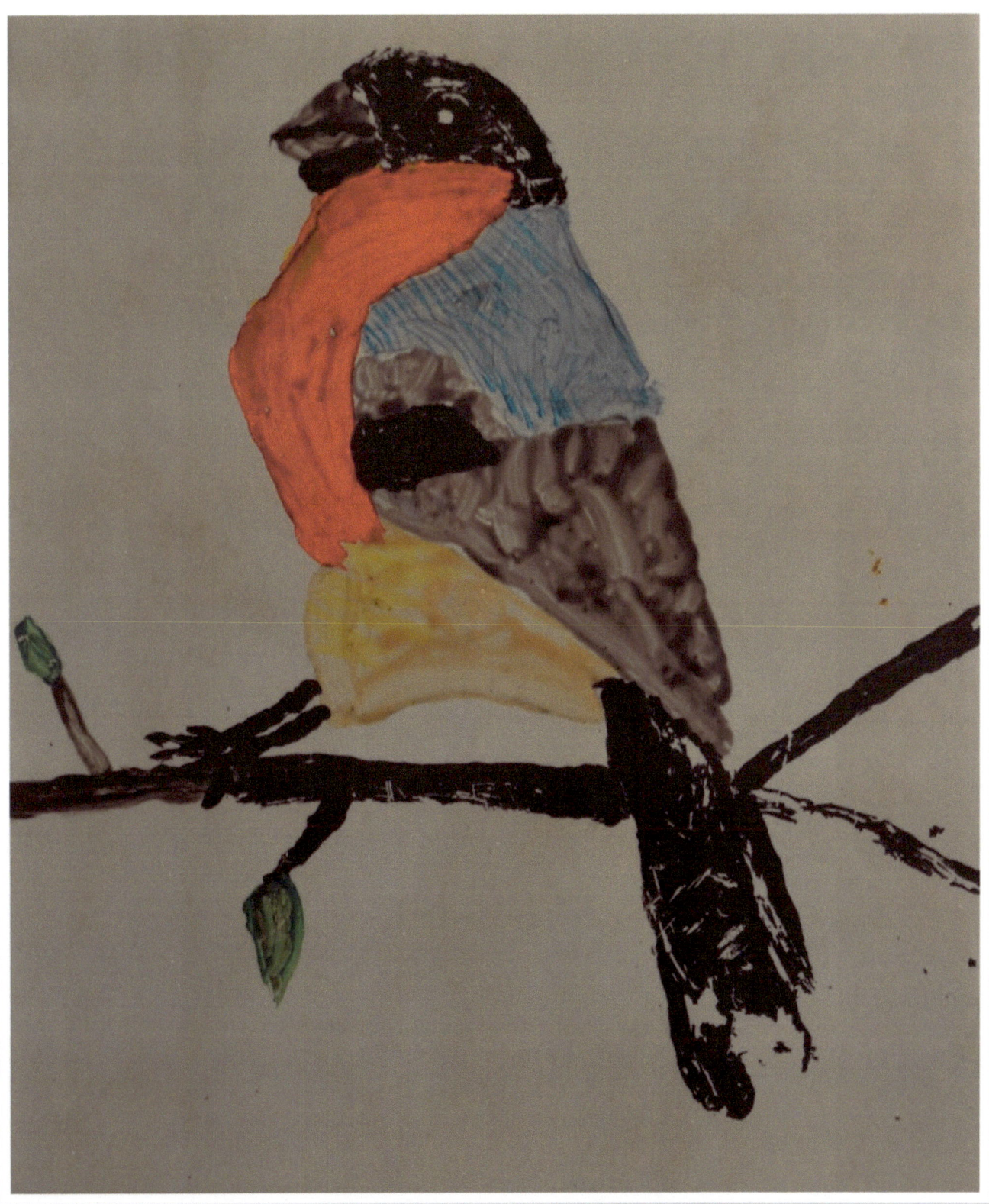

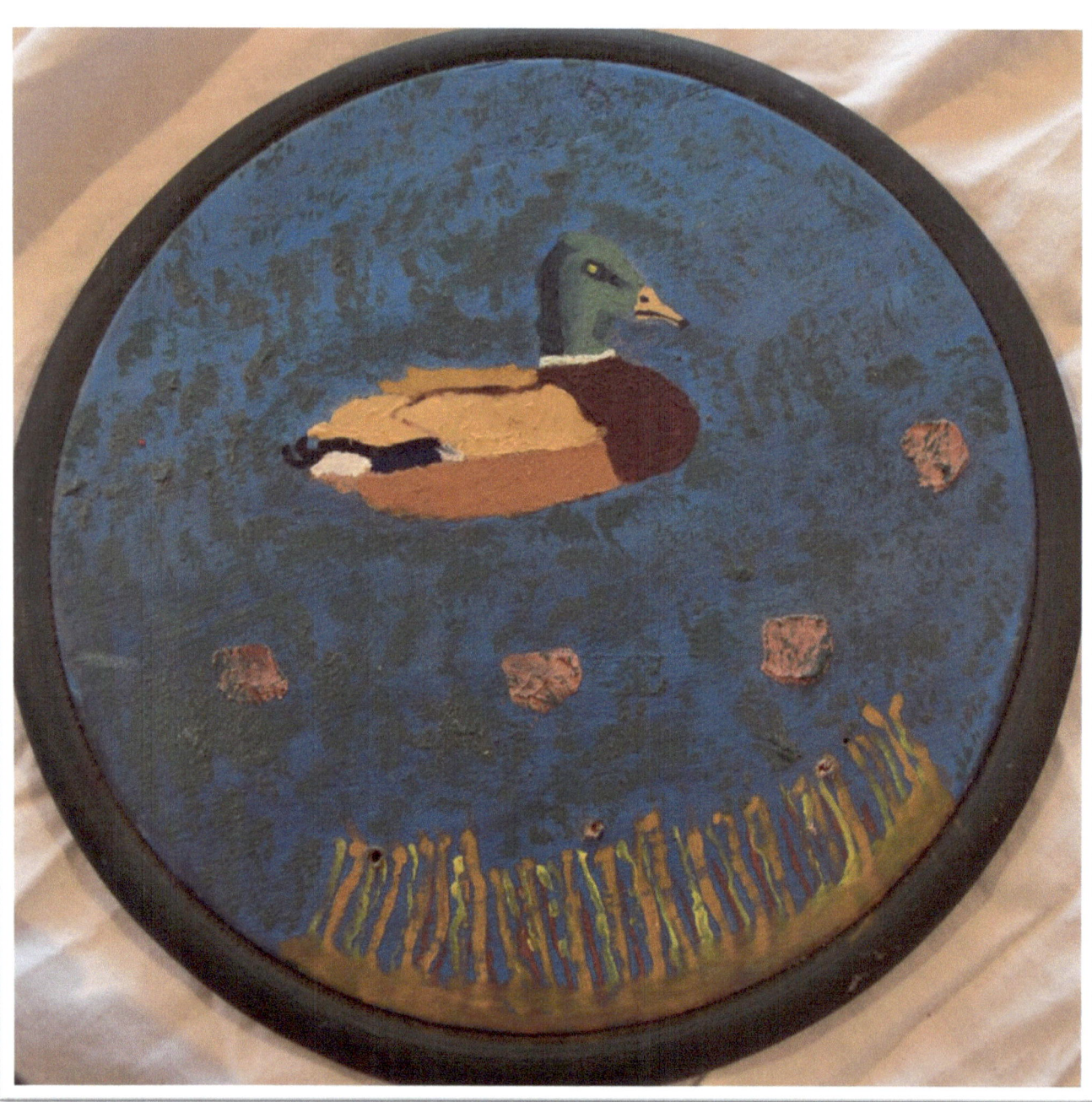

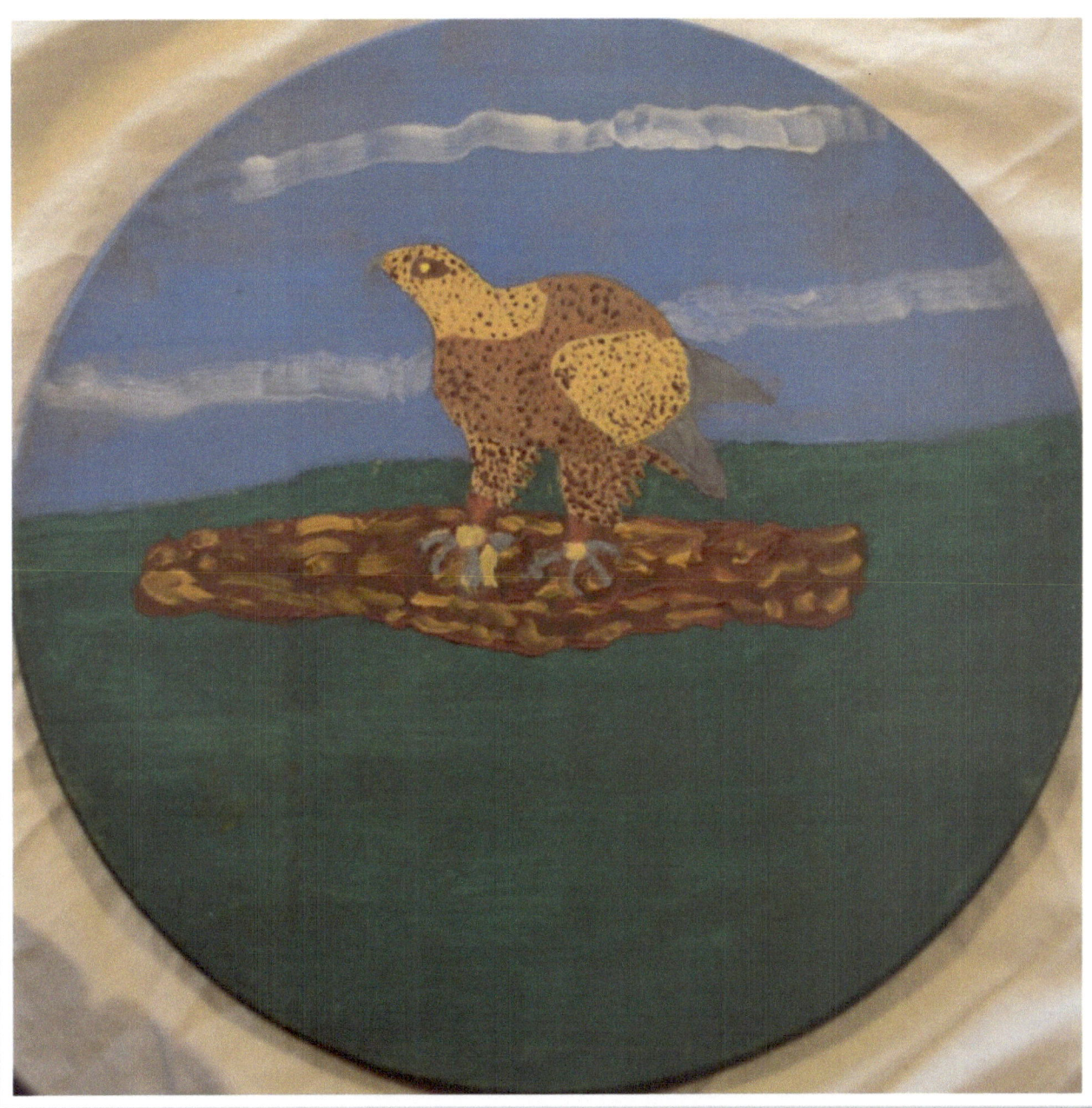

4. Bridges

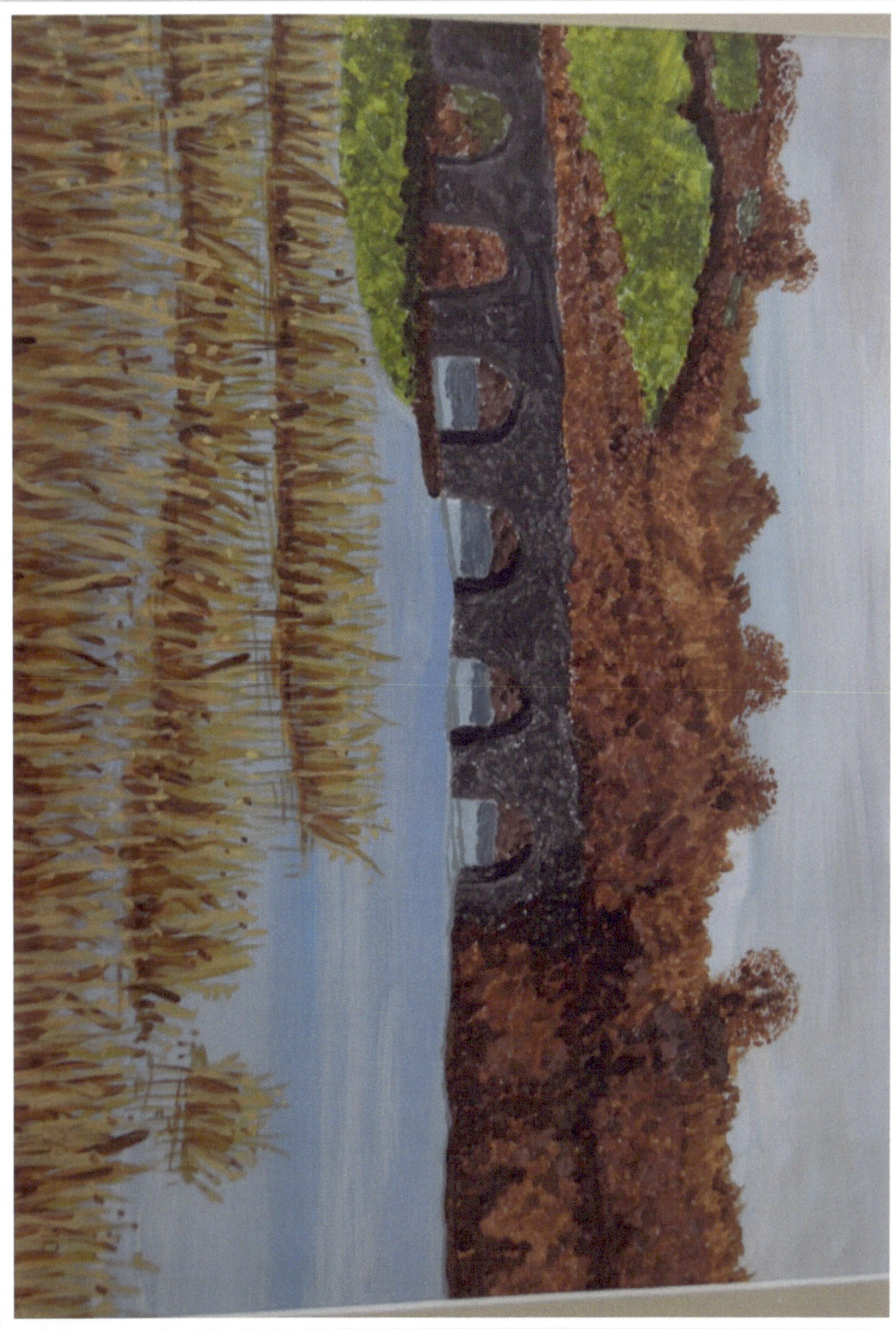

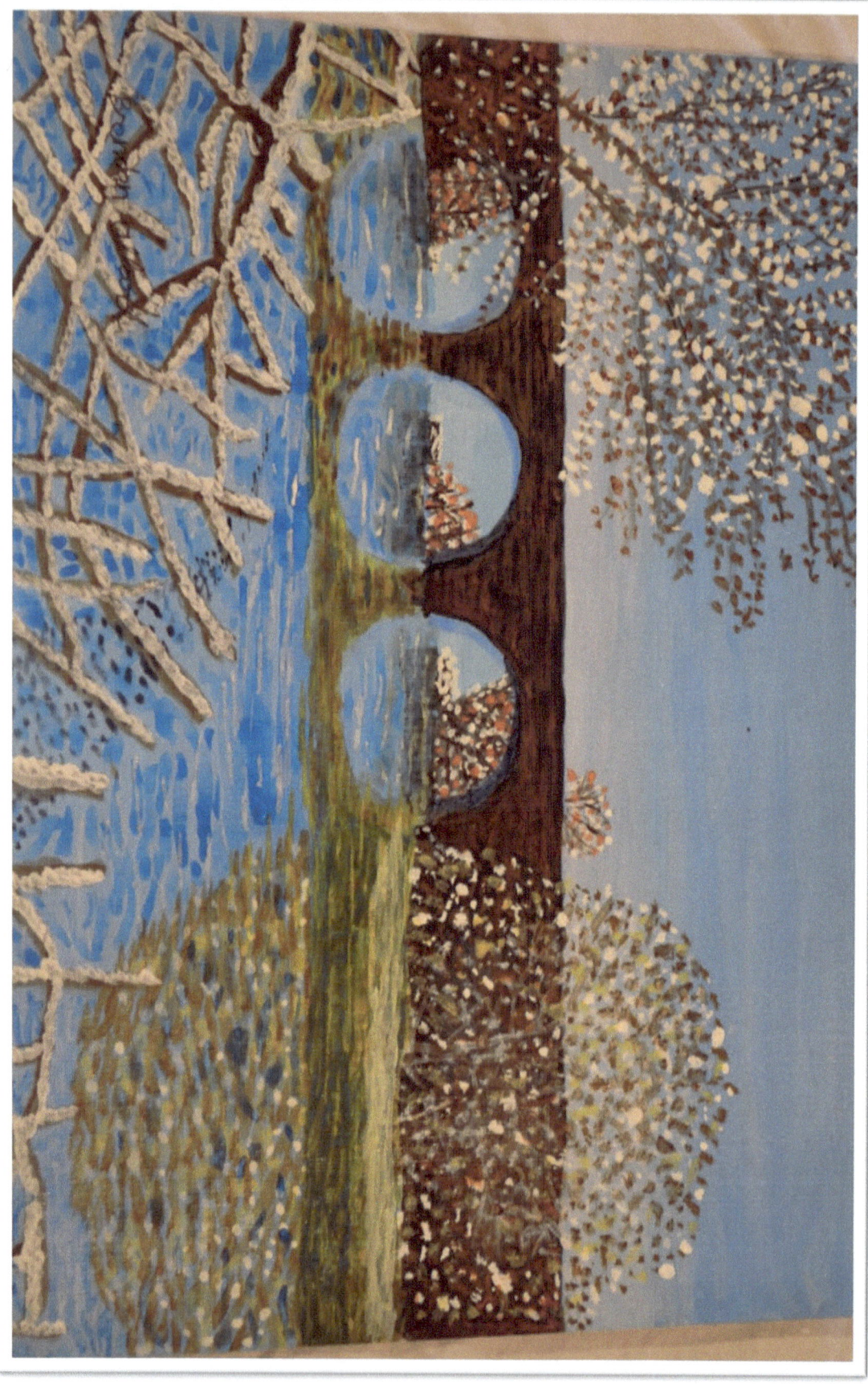

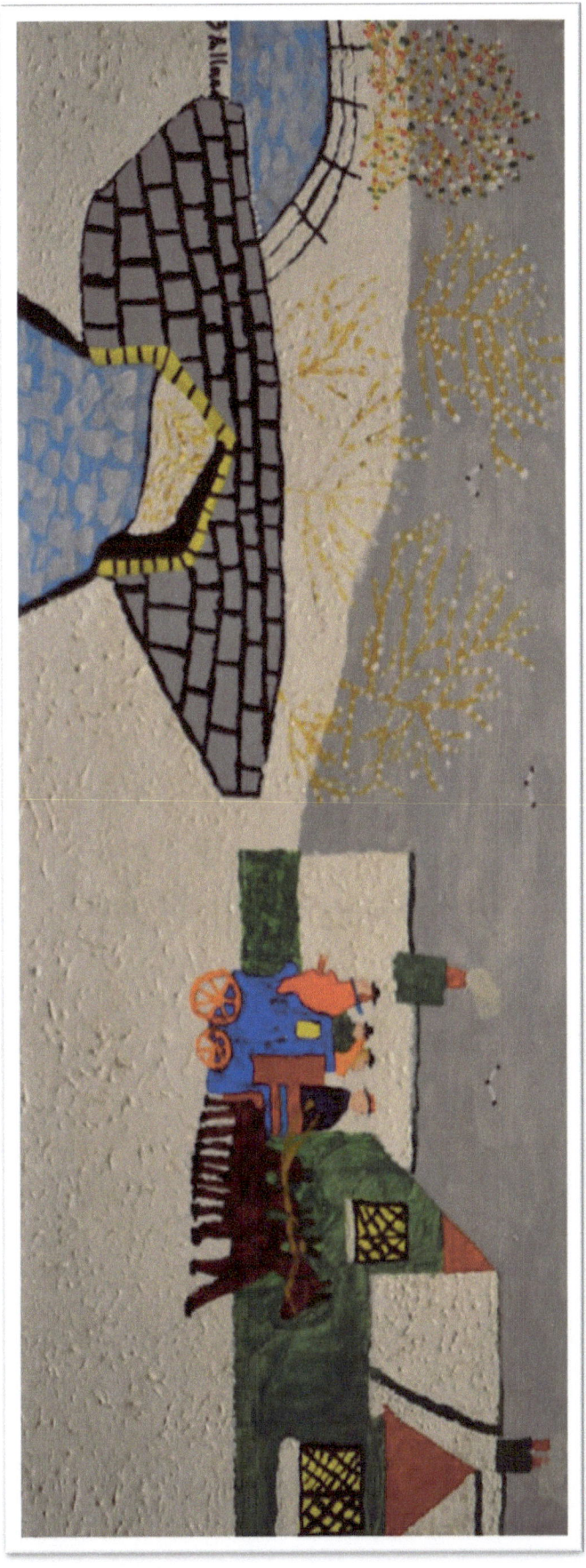

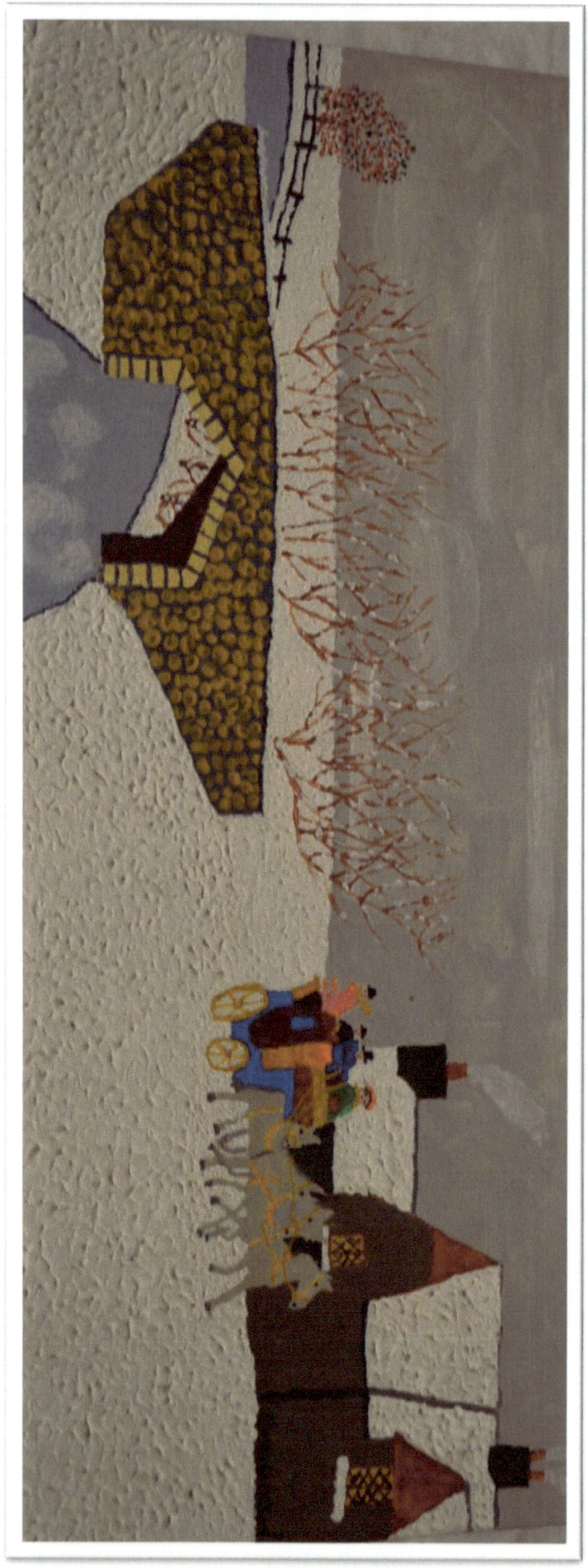

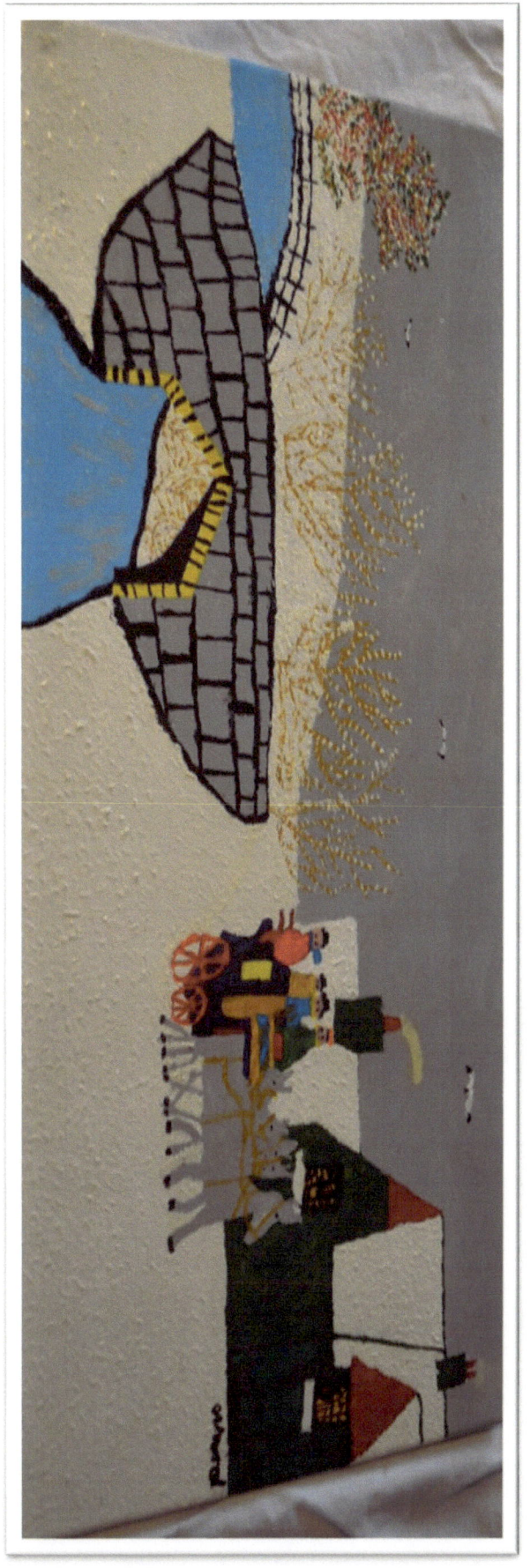

5. Seascapes

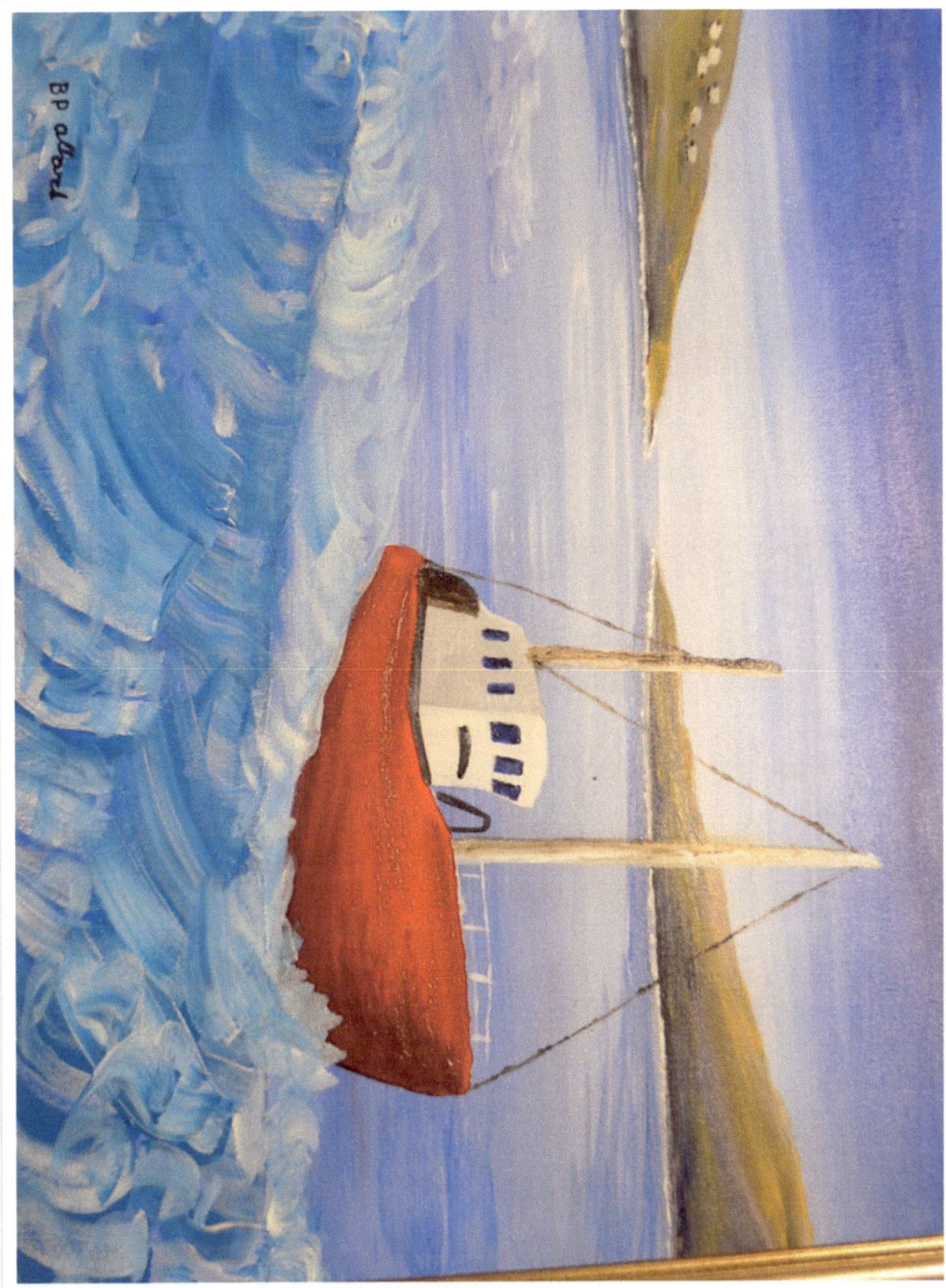

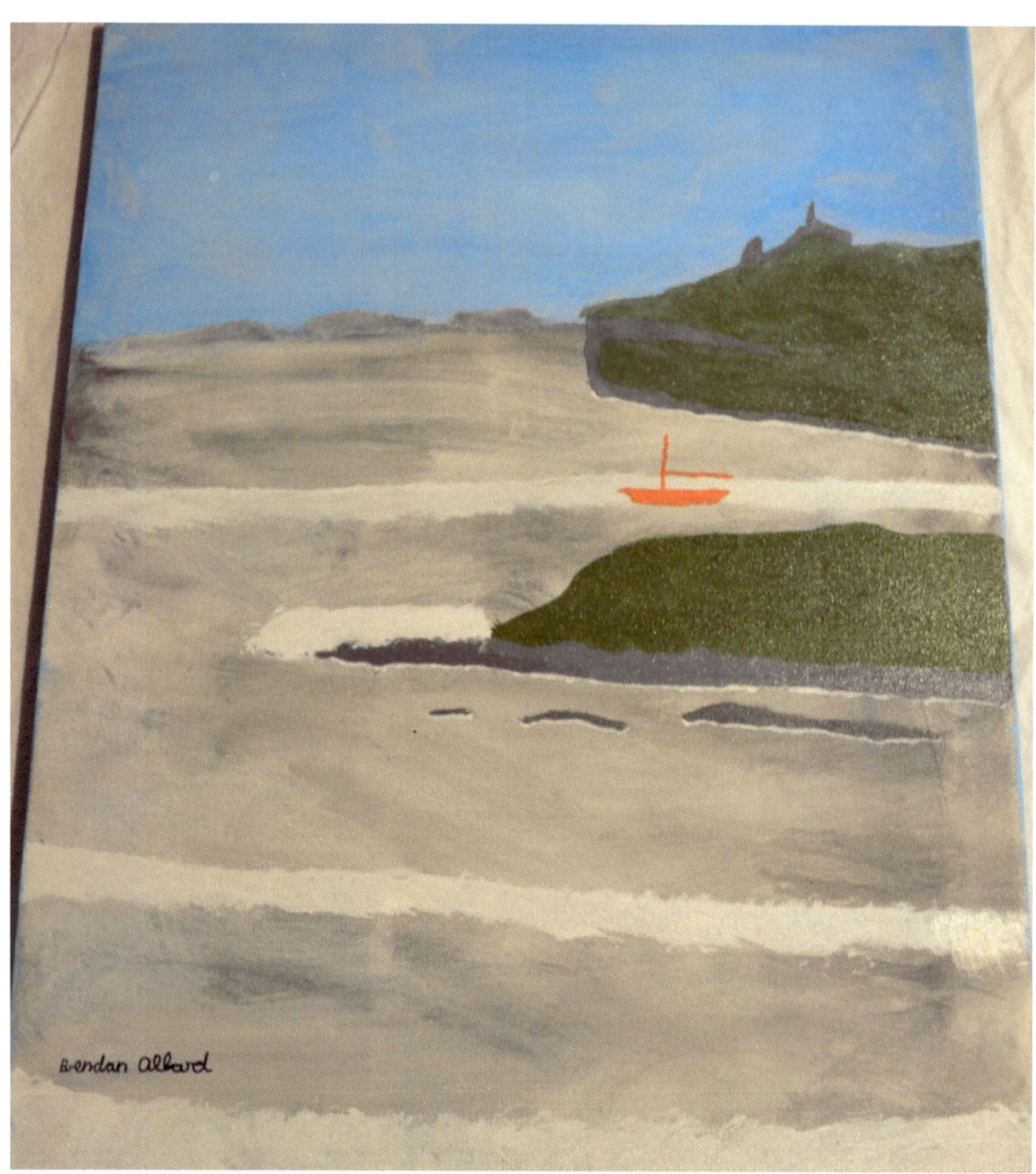

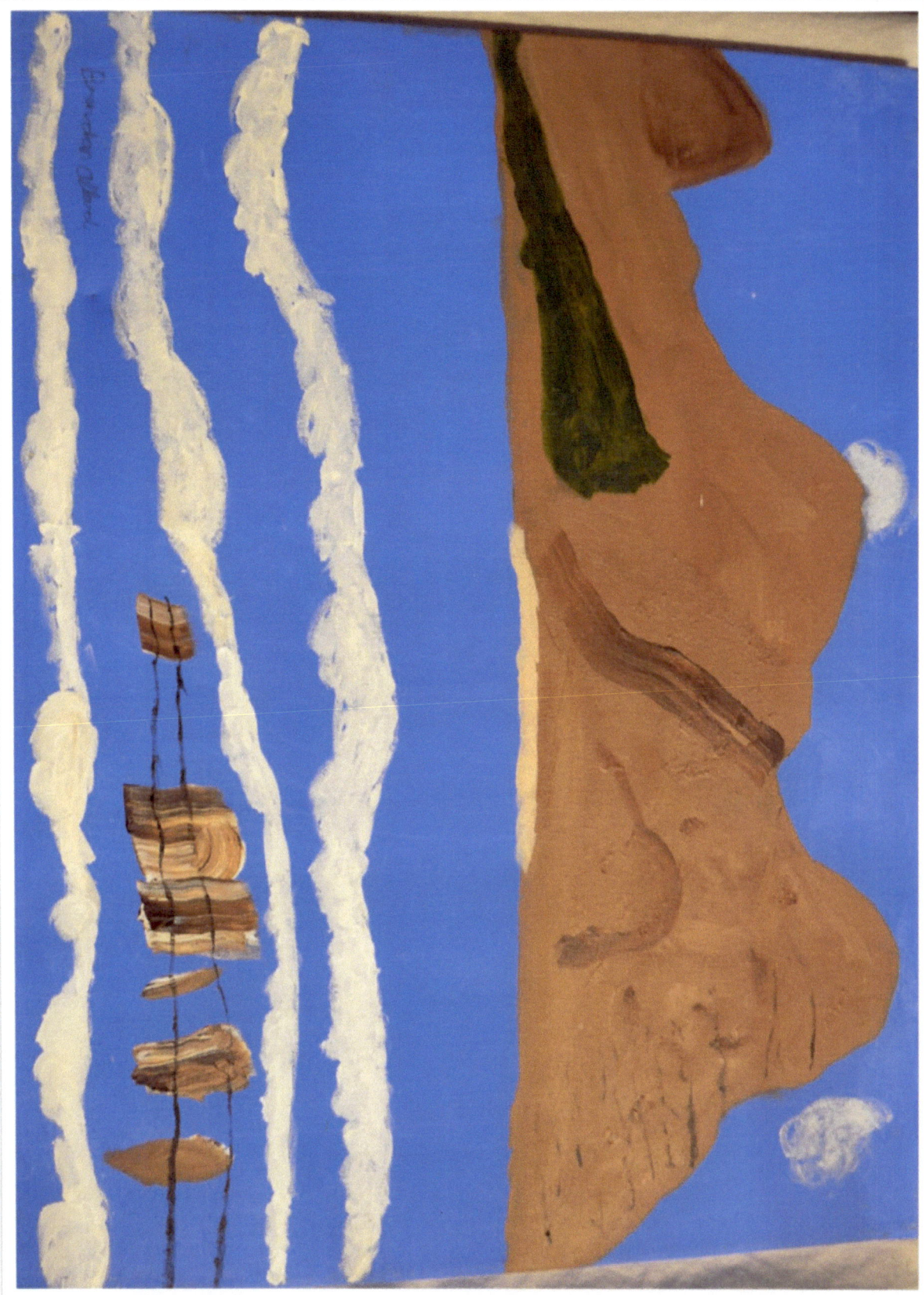

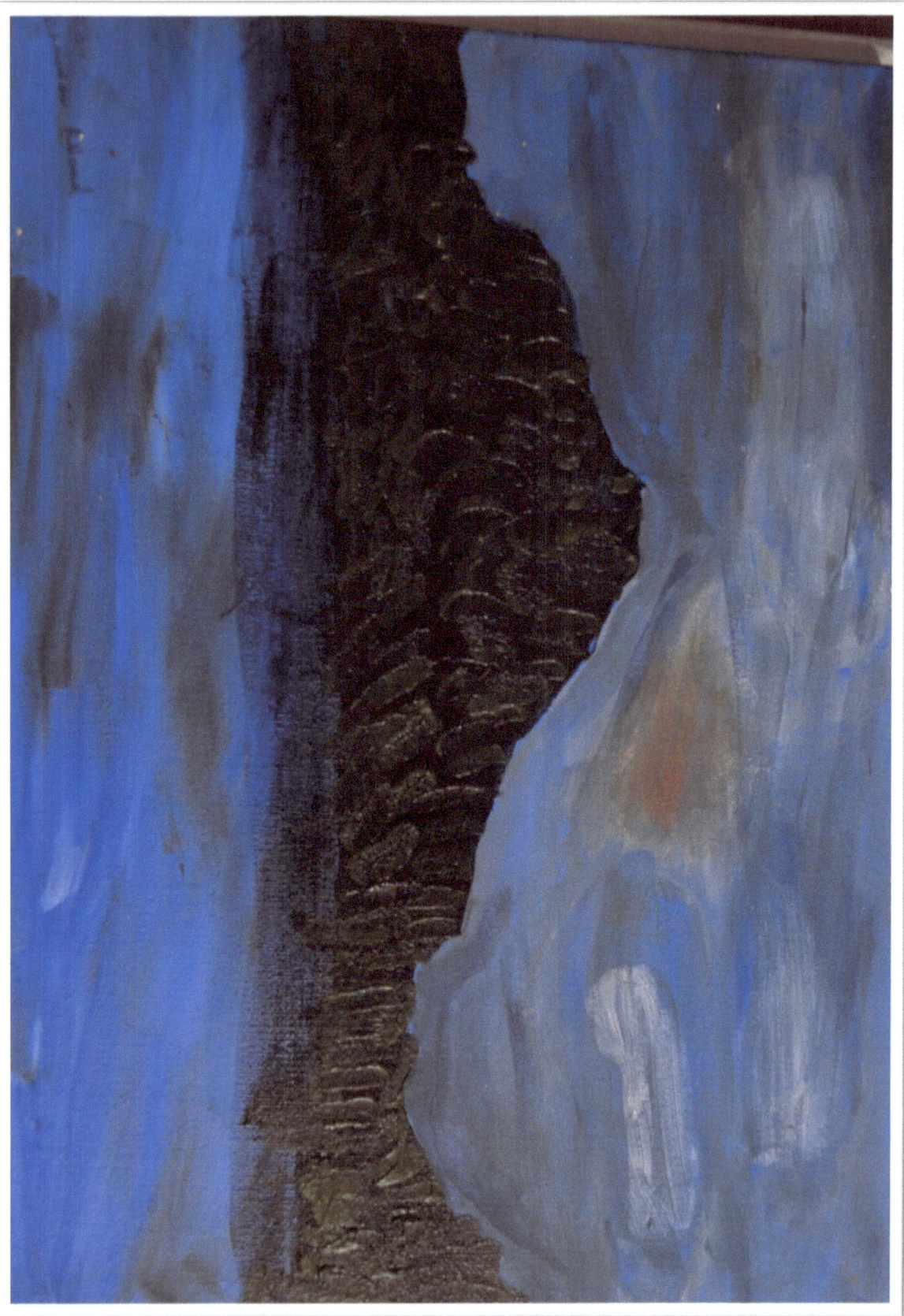

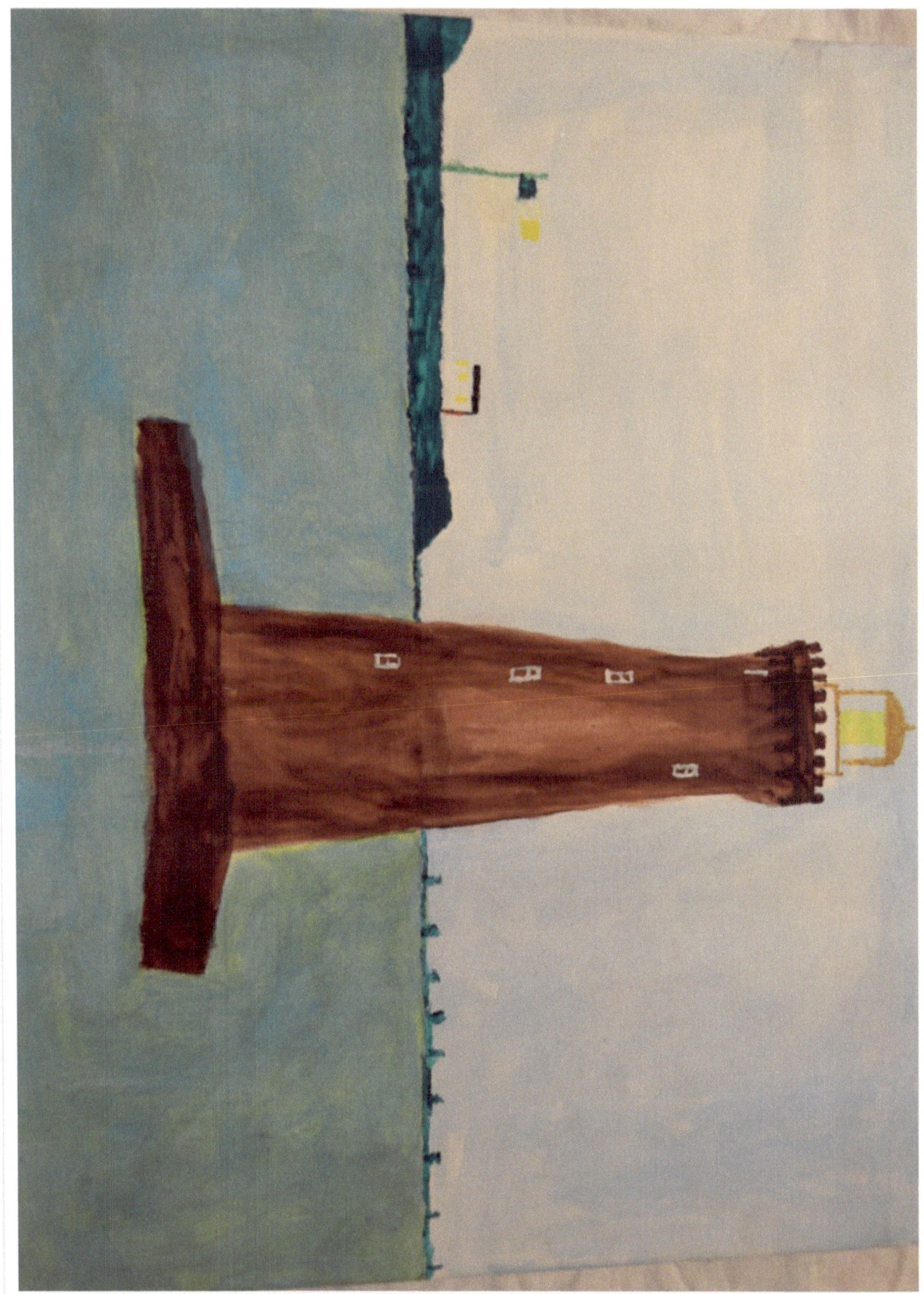

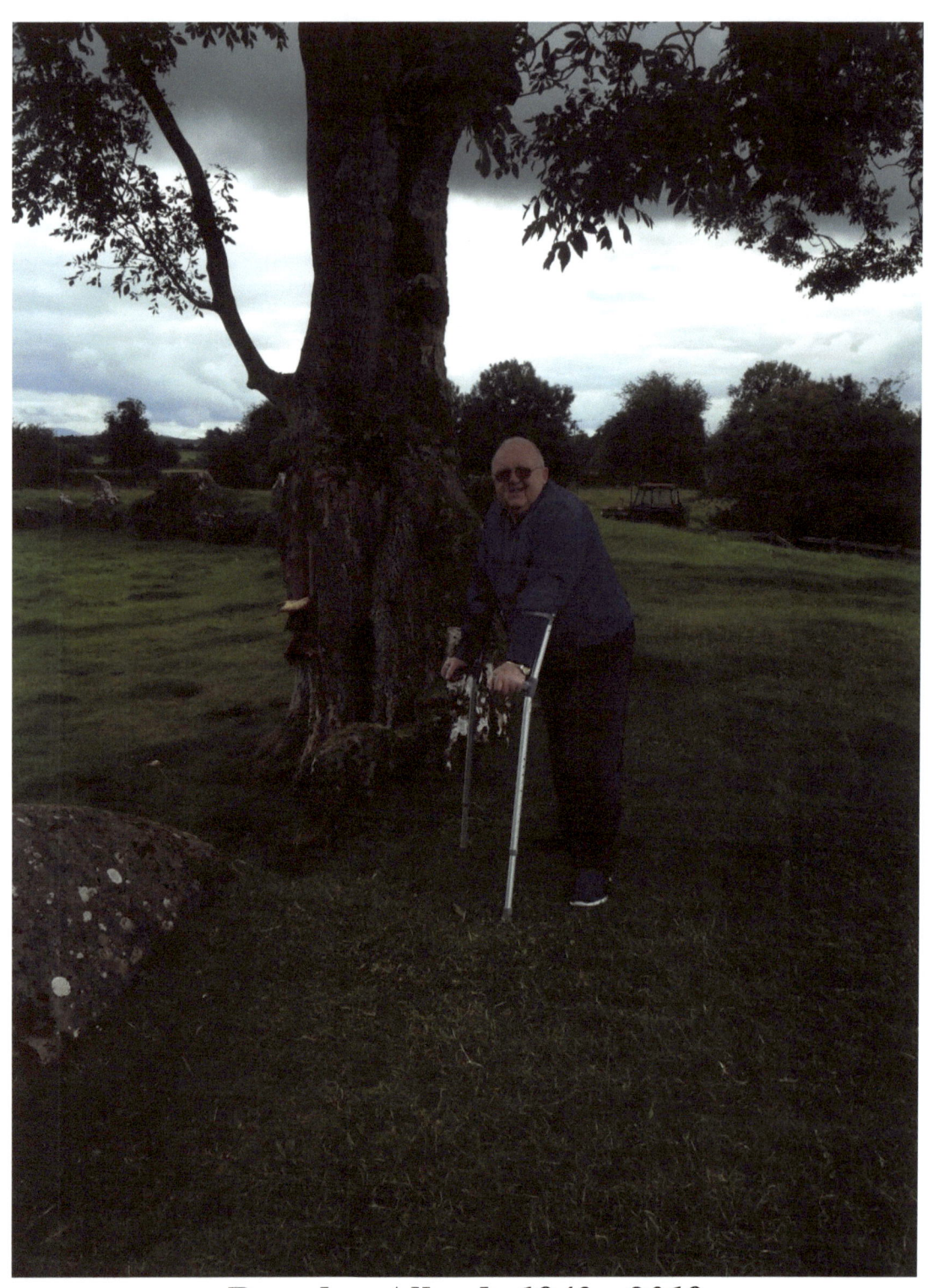

Brendan Allard: *1943 - 2019*

www.ingramcontent.com/pod-product-compliance
Lightning Source LLC
Chambersburg PA
CBHW040411220526
45473CB00004B/1206